Re: Stocks

Optimize Your Returns with the Sparkman Stock Selection System (S4)

by

Roy Sparkman & Travis Sparkman

ISBN (e-Book): 979-8-89604-600-4

ISBN (Paperback): 979-8-89604-601-1

ISBN (Hardback): 979-8-89604-602-8

Table of Contents

Dedication

To Alexa, my long-suffering wife of 48 years who has put up with me throughout my career and listened patiently as I droned on about the market and investments. You are still the beautiful girl I started dating in college and the smartest person I have ever known.

-Roy

To Alicia—your love and support have been the quiet strength behind every bold move.

-Travis

About the Authors

Roy Sparkman Founded Sparkman Private Wealth Management and acts as a consultant to Independent Financial Advisors. His career as a Financial Advisor, Branch Manager and Owner of a private wealth management company spans 5 decades. He is also a CERTIFIED FINANCIAL PLANNER® Professional. Roy has worked for a Fortune 500 corporation and has owned two small businesses. This experience helps him relate to a wide variety of investors. As a graduate of Texas Tech University, he is a proud Red Raider. He lives on a lake in the beautiful Texas Hill Country with his wife, Alexa. They have three grown sons, Ryan, Travis, and Will, and 9 grandchildren.

Travis Sparkman began his career in the Financial Industry as a child in his dad's office, where he ran errands, eventually becoming an apprentice. After graduating with a degree in Computer Technology from Howard Payne University and becoming a Financial Advisor helped solidify and computerize the investment system that Roy had been developing over the years. Since taking over Sparkman Wealth Management, he has built it to the company it is today. He and his wife, Alicia, live in Austin, Texas, and have 3 children.

Acknowledgement

I want to acknowledge the help that my wife, Alexa, gave as she proofread the book and offered changes. Thanks to my sons for giving me a plethora of stories to tell. A particular thanks to Travis for joining the business and helping to develop it. Now that you are the owner, I can't wait to see how you can grow it further. Also, thanks to my long-time Operations manager of 27 years, Leticia Cofield, for helping me build the company.

-Roy

Writing this book has been a deeply personal and rewarding journey, and I am profoundly grateful to those who have supported me along the way.

First and foremost, I want to thank my incredible wife, Alicia, whose unwavering love, patience, and encouragement have been the foundation of everything I do. Her belief in this project—and in me—has meant more than words can express.

To my children, Jordan, Kora, and Tessa: you are my inspiration and my joy. This book is, in many ways, a reflection of the values I hope to pass on to you—curiosity, discipline, and the courage to think independently. Thank you for reminding me every day why legacy matters.

To my father, thank you for bringing me into the family business. Your patience, wisdom, and persistence laid the foundation for everything this book represents. I'm grateful for the lessons, the laughs, and the spreadsheets.

To Sydney Michna, a great Operations Manager—thank you for keeping the wheels turning even when I'm off chasing charts and chapters.

Preface

Because you are reading this book, you are probably either looking for a more logical system of buying stocks or are a new investor trying to learn how to get started. Either way, we think this short, easy-to-read book will give you a clear, elegant answer to your needs.

The idea of this book has been rolling around in my feeble head for years and was originally conceived as I pondered the question of how to explain to my three sons and grandkids the investment strategy that I have developed during my investment career. The metamorphoses of the strategy came about over the past 40 years, from beginning as a Financial Advisor to becoming a CERTIFIED FINANCIAL PLANNER® Professional and progressing to Private Wealth Management. Over those years, I attended a lot of Investment conferences, listened to a lot of advice (both correct and incorrect), took multiple courses, studied for hundreds of hours for various long certification tests (the CFP® test alone was 10 hours long), and went through a lot of trials and errors in my own investment accounts. I will say that I learned more from the errors made than from any other form of training. Why is it that mistakes are better teachers than successes? I was determined to help my sons learn how to invest without repeating the same painful learning experiences, and so I began developing a technique that has helped me and countless clients grow their net worth.

Now, one of my sons, Travis, who was my business partner for several years and recently took over the company, has been instrumental in the development, improvement, and computerization of this Sparkman Stock Selection System (S4).

I feel your potential for investment returns will improve as you systematically use the principles described.

-Roy Sparkman

I grew up in the investment business. I can remember sitting on my dad's lap while he looked up stock quotes. I had no idea what he was doing, though. Later, when we were a little older, sometimes my brothers and I would watch a little CNBC on the TV with my dad, and he would point out the stocks he was buying for clients. As the symbols crossed the screen, he would say "yay" or "boo" depending on whether they were up or down. He would also try to give us the most elementary explanation of his reasons for buying a stock. Sometimes I even understood. When I was older, occasionally he would take me to his office. At that time, a broker had to write an order ticket by hand and take it to a lady called the wire operator. When I was there, he would hand me the ticket, and I would walk it across the office and hand it to the wire operator. I always wanted to be an investor. When the opportunity arose for me to become a Financial Advisor in my dad's business, I jumped at it. I spent years studying the stock market and investments under the mentorship of dear old dad. I also began, through my education in computer technology, to take his stock selection system and develop a program to do most of the work for him. Up until that point, he had been doing all the work by hand. Now the worm has turned. The business is mine and growing, and he works for me as a consultant.

We have decided to put the backbone of the Sparkman Stock Selection System (S4) into this book to help you understand the process used. We think this will help investors have a better knowledge of and therefore feel more comfortable with the stock purchases they make. So, whether you do all the work yourself or let your Financial Advisor make the investments for you or recommend them to you, if this system is used, you will understand the process.

-Travis Sparkman

Chapter 1

The Journey to Stock Brokerage: A Personal Story

In the Orwellian year of 1984, I was hired to be trained as a stockbroker with the firm of Dean Witter Reynolds, which has since been absorbed by Morgan Stanley. Dean Witter was a very nice, successful California-based company. The year before, it had been bought out by the great American retailer, Sears. The price was rumored to have cost Sears only one day's cash flow. After the purchase, Sears set up kiosks in each of their stores, out of which Dean Witter could operate some of its branches. Thus, the joke was that certain Dean Witter brokers who worked out of these kiosks sold stocks and socks. After many months of studying and training in our branch office in Austin, Texas, a difficult 7-hour test, and a month of intense training at our headquarters, I was deemed licensed and ready to hit the streets as a professional Investment Advisor. I remember sitting down at my nice, clean, real-life professional desk in my little cubicle inside our main downtown branch on the first day back from training and asking myself, "What do I do now?" To those who have seen the 1987 film, Wall Street, there is a scene in which the branch manager of a large brokerage firm hands the phone book to the new broker and tells him that every one of his potential clients is in this book, and all he must do is call everyone in it to find his clients and build his book of business. My first day was like that scene, but the manager explained how to refine the list to increase the odds of calling someone willing to listen to my investment idea. Everyone was to be told about a municipal bond portfolio, called a unit trust, that at the time paid an unbelievable, astonishing tax-free interest rate of 11%. Did I say that the interest it paid was tax-free? Tax Free! Who could pass that up? Amazingly, a lot of people could pass it up. But luckily, enough investors were interested and bought the unit trusts that I was able to start and grow my new book of clients. It was recommended that I make 100 dials per day, on the telephone I grew to hate, to people I didn't know, telling them about the same investment. If my memory serves me, inflation was around 12% though, so even with the giant yield of the unit trust, the current real return was negative 1% (11% interest yield minus 12% inflation), so this didn't seem like a great long-term strategy for a young broker trying to build his book. At least, these bond portfolios had the potential to increase in value as interest rates came down. But I took the job to be a stockbroker. I wanted to learn how to analyze and buy and sell stocks for clients because I was convinced that the easiest way to build wealth was to invest in them. The problem was that I had no idea how to do this. The instructors in my training classes had conveniently avoided teaching us about how to analyze individual stocks, opting for showing us packaged products like the aforementioned unit trusts and mutual funds. Not that there is anything wrong with these products (almost every investment has its place), but I really felt like there would always be a need for someone who could understand stocks and who could explain them to others.

So, I went to the "experts" that I knew. I decided to ask the wise, old, more experienced brokers in the office which stocks they buy and why. I don't remember which stocks they were and the myriad reasons for liking them, but I do remember that each one of them went down as I watched and tried to find at least one that would work. Maybe the experts don't have a crystal ball.

Still trying to find the elusive system to find the perfect equity investment, I read about some famous investors who used math to figure out stocks that were selling at discounts to their perceived value. This is called fundamental analysis. Now, that made sense in my neophyte mind. I have always liked math and, at times, even showed some skill in the area. If there was a way to calculate a company's value and then buy it at a lower price, a client would be bound to make money. It turns out that you can find some stocks at a discounted price. Unfortunately, a lot of investors must find such stocks at the same time and begin to buy them in enormous quantities before the price actually begins to move. Most of these companies were not well-known. So even after finding them, they seemed to induce a deep sleep in people until they were forgotten or sold off from portfolios because of sheer boredom.

What I needed were stocks that were moving up. Makes sense, doesn't it? I was introduced to the world of technical analysis and charts. According to the technical experts, all an investor must do is find stocks whose trading charts are moving up or look like some sort of special picture, like a cup with a handle or an upside-down man (called a reverse head and shoulders pattern), or any of an assortment of other patterns, and you could find a winner. And sometimes, if the stars all lined up and the moon was in the correct place, there was a small percentage of these stocks that actually did go up. What I found was that if I looked at these charts for too long, I could make a chart look like anything in my mind's eye, and who's to say that the current picture that it appeared to be forming was just the end of a nice run and a new negative formation wasn't beginning? Plus, it turns out that even if the chart is very pretty, if the company itself isn't making a profit, the chart can turn down quickly. So, those investors who were chasing the momentum of the stock chart can lose money if level heads prevail. The stock can pull back because the fickle buyers have moved on to the next latest and greatest stock chart.

I also came to realize that users of fundamental analysis and advocates of technical analysis did not like each other's philosophies of investing. There seemed to be very few analysts who used both disciplines. East is east, and west is west, and never the twain shall meet. I studied both sides of the arguments and wondered if there might be some way to combine the two methods to find a better method for an ordinary guy like me to pick great stocks to create successful portfolios. Couldn't there be a logical, conservative way to potentially make a decent profit?

I think there is. Over the years, through trial and error, I started to piece together the above lessons and develop the strategy that we now call the Sparkman Stock Selection System (S4). The following is a piece-by-piece method of the system that Travis and I have developed to locate and buy prime stocks as investments, and an explanation of why we make the decisions. We believe the process is logical, conservative, and elegant when used consistently.

-Roy

Chapter 2

The Power of Investment: Turning Savings into Wealth

Why do we need to invest? We all have goals that we would like to achieve in life. For those who are still working, the most common goal is to be able to retire without a substantial decrease in lifestyle. Your job needs to provide a living for your family right now and provide the investment seeds to grow and blossom into a future income for an older person with your name several years down the road. Other people may have the goal of sending their children or grandchildren to college. Still others may want to travel. One goal we regularly see is the ability to give more to their church or charities. Here is the cold, hard reality: Unless you are in the enviable group of the highest earners in the world, we believe that you have realized that you can't just save your way to wealth. A savings account or even CDs will probably not get you to your goals.

The best way to look at your assets is to see each dollar as an employee. You want these employees to be working for you. The great thing is that you don't have to pay these workers. They pay you. All you need to do is keep an eye on them to make sure they are still working. Before you begin to invest, these assets are probably just sitting in a savings account. Your employees are just sleeping. They aren't actively working for you. It's fine to let some of them sleep, so that you will have cash when you need it, but the majority need to be working for you. Put them to work. Invest them. Even the Bible encourages investing. Jesus tells the parable of the servants whose master is going on a long journey. He gives each servant some money to care for while he is gone. When he comes back, he asks the servants about the money. The ones who invested the funds and made them grow were praised and rewarded, but the one who basically buried the money in a tin can and made no profits was scolded and called wicked and lazy. The master said the "least" he could have done was put it in a bank and earn interest on it. That tells us that we need to be active in our investments. Put your employees to work. Obviously, we feel the best way to do this is to invest in stocks. If we didn't, we wouldn't be writing this book.

So, why stocks? There are several asset classes of investments in which you can get involved. Theoretically, you have the potential to make a profit on them all... over time.

What are these alternative classes of investments? Here are a few. The assets we will look at are stocks, U.S.

Government Bonds, Corporate Bonds, Gold, and Real Estate. We will look at them in reverse order.

Real Estate

Real estate represents a solid, tangible asset with inherently limited supply, making it fundamentally different from paper investments. Since everyone needs shelter, there's a consistent underlying demand that provides a foundation for the investment's value proposition. Property ownership offers dual income potential through rental yields and capital appreciation, particularly when investing in areas experiencing economic growth or demographic shifts. The tangible nature of real estate also provides psychological comfort to investors who prefer assets they can see and touch, though this comes with responsibilities like maintenance, property management, and dealing with tenant issues. But real estate can fluctuate in value and can be illiquid at times.

Corporate Bonds

Corporate bonds function as debt instruments where investors essentially loan money to companies in exchange for regular interest payments and principal repayment at maturity. Well-established companies with strong credit ratings offer relatively predictable returns, making these bonds attractive for income-focused investors seeking steady cash flow. The bond's market value fluctuates inversely with interest rate movements, creating opportunities for capital gains if rates decline, but also potential paper losses if rates rise. However, investors who hold bonds to maturity can expect to receive their full principal back regardless of interim price fluctuations, assuming the company remains solvent.

U.S. Government Bonds

U.S. Treasury securities are considered the gold standard of safety in the investment world, backed by the full faith and credit of the federal government. This supreme safety comes at the cost of lower yields compared to corporate bonds, reflecting the trade-off between risk and return that governs all investing. Like corporate bonds, Treasury securities experience price volatility in response to interest rate changes, but their government backing virtually eliminates default risk. These instruments serve as portfolio anchors during turbulent times and provide a benchmark against which other investments are measured.

Gold

Gold has served as a store of value and medium of exchange for millennia, earning its reputation as a hedge against currency debasement and economic uncertainty. Its appeal extends beyond investment purposes to jewelry, industrial applications, and cultural significance in many societies worldwide. However, gold generates no income through dividends or interest, making its total return dependent entirely on price appreciation driven by factors like inflation expectations, geopolitical tensions, and currency fluctuations. The precious metal's price can be surprisingly volatile despite its reputation for stability, sometimes moving dramatically based on market sentiment and macroeconomic forces that can seem disconnected from its fundamental value.

Stocks

Stock ownership represents claims on the future earnings and assets of businesses, offering investors participation in the long-term growth of the economy through individual companies. Dividend-paying stocks can provide income that often grows over time as successful companies increase their payouts, while growth stocks reinvest earnings to fuel expansion and potentially dramatic price appreciation. The performance of individual stocks depends heavily on company-specific factors like management quality, competitive position, profitability of the company, and industry trends, making stock selection and diversification crucial considerations. This asset class historically provides the highest long-term returns but comes with significant volatility and the risk of permanent loss if companies fail or industries become obsolete.

Now let's look at the cold, hard facts of investment return over the years. In her article of April 3, 2024, in Money, Dorothy Neufold clearly lays out the historical returns of these assets between 1923 and 1970. During that time, a $100 investment in corporate bonds would have grown to $7,750, U.S., by reinvesting and compounding the interest payments. Government 10-year bonds would have grown to $2,286, gold would have grown to $5,545, and real estate to $1,542. These all seem like decent returns. But now compare that to the stock market returns. During the same period, the $100 invested in the stock market in 1970 would have grown to $22,419, eclipsing the other asset classes.

This article used the S&P 500 plus dividends to represent stocks, Corporate Bonds were represented by Baa corporate bonds, U.S. government bonds were represented by 10-year Treasury Bonds, and real estate was represented by the Case-Shiller Home Price Index.

Another reason that we like investing in stocks is the liquidity. If an emergency or special situation creates a sudden need for cash, shares of stock can be sold immediately, and the proceeds can be used to settle the trade within one day. One does not have to sell one's entire position of a stock, just enough shares to cover the situation. If, on the other hand, an investor is heavy in real estate and an emergency occurs, the investor may have to sell off an entire house, apartment complex, or office building to free up the cash. They may also have to wait for months for the real estate sale to close, assuming they can find a buyer at the time.

We know that we will now begin receiving emails, letters, and phone calls telling us that we don't know what we are talking about and telling us of the great returns the person has made on real estate. If you are in one of the country's great growth regions, that's great! There are numerous areas that have experienced flat returns or even declines. The returns in this example, however, are national. We are not trying to shed a bad light on real estate. We both own real estate, but we still believe there is a myth about this asset class that makes it seem safer. We believe the main reason for this misconception is that real estate owners don't receive a monthly statement showing the exact value of their asset. Stock investors receive regular account statements and can view their stocks to see real-time prices for each equity held. Real estate owners would probably be surprised to see the fluctuations in the value of their holdings on a month-by-month basis.

A unique quality of working with stocks is the variety of assets that can be bought within equities. Let's say that you understand the need to own stocks in your portfolio, but you still like the idea of owning other assets. No problem. If you like real estate, you can invest in REITs (Real Estate Investment Trusts). These are companies that invest in various real estate assets but are traded as securities on the stock markets. They usually pay high dividends and have potential appreciation. If you like gold, there are ETFs (Electronically Traded Funds) that own gold to back each share of the security. There are also ETFs and closed-end funds that buy bonds. If one is of the more speculative bent, some ETFs buy Bitcoins and other coin-based products. If you have ever wanted to own an oil well, look at the large oil exploration companies or EFTs. You can theoretically buy very small positions in thousands of wells by buying their stocks.

We are not saying that you should put all your money into any one of these investments. We always recommend a diversified portfolio and only buy assets when a buy signal appears per our strategy. We are simply trying to show investors the different asset types that can be bought in the equity market.

Why the Sparkman Stock Selection System (S4)? We have developed our approach to finding growing stocks and buying them at an optimal time to help investors get a head start on the market in general. If you picture two planes ready for take-off. We want the plane that will get off the runway and into smooth air the quickest. Since developing our system years ago, we have found that we can obtain better optimization and performance in our portfolios. If that interests you, we can begin learning the process. Read on.

The Process

The first step in our process for successful stock investing is to compile a list of publicly traded companies whose products or services you regularly use or have a good reputation for creating quality products. It really doesn't matter if they are a manufacturer, a consumer products company, a service business, a software or hardware company, a restaurant chain, or an energy company. A quality company is the only requirement. By looking at the additions to the list in that way, you will naturally develop a diversified list of companies, both large and small.

Now that we have our list of companies to regularly monitor, we need to agree that not all companies are a buy at any one time, and they aren't all a sell at any one time. Some companies are too expensive to buy at some point, and some are at too deep a discount to their value to justify selling at certain times. So, our next task is to begin our analysis to determine which companies are good buys at a given time. This is where the heart of our proprietary process lies. Begin with fundamental analysis. We do this first by selecting the P/E (price to earnings ratio) of the company and relating that to its projected earnings growth rate (the P/E/G rate). After these calculations have been performed, we have a pretty good idea of which stocks look relatively inexpensive and have growth potential. But potential isn't action. The next step is to determine the optimum time to buy that stock by attempting to maximize the return while potentially minimizing the risk, or at least feeling comfortable with the risk. That is when we use charts on the stock and look for specific changes in patterns that we consider buy signals. This is called technical analysis. That is where you will learn when to pull the trigger and begin to buy the stock.

The selling process is basically a mirror image of the buying process, but in reverse.

Each step of this entire strategy will be discussed in greater detail in the following chapters.

After that, we will discuss a strategy for buying interesting securities called closed-end funds.

Chapter 3

Creating Your Stock Universe

Now it is time to start the fun part. We have found, over the years, that it was becoming ineffective and inefficient for us to continually try to find the next hot new stock that would shoot skyward like a Fourth of July bottle rocket. Even with grandiose dreams of finding a stock that would make our clients and ourselves rich in just a few months, the reality is that this elusive stock is next to impossible to find. As we found a new stock in which to invest, it started to feel as though we were asking a perfect stranger for her hand in marriage. We still needed to get to know her and find out if her personality was really what we were wishing for. We spent a lot of time researching unfamiliar stocks. And then, much like in F. Scott Fitzgerald's The Diamond as Big as the Ritz, we found that the optimum stocks for our investment needs were in our own backyard. They were already scattered in our various portfolios. These were companies that we already knew, liked their personalities, and were comfortable with their eccentricities. All we had to do was to consolidate them into a universe from which we could pick the various stocks that we felt this would have the highest probabilities of being the best buys on a given day. We were already familiar with these companies and how they moved. For the most part, we knew the good, the bad, and the ugly of these investments. So, we refined our list and narrowed it down to a population of approximately 150 friends who are now waiting for the opportunity to work for our cause. This became our universe of stocks from which we could make our daily buys or sales. Once this universe was established, the time we spent looking for the next great investment was drastically reduced.

We recommend using the same strategy to find your ideal portfolios. To begin your list, this is what we recommend: follow your money! Look in your pantry at home. Which products are in it? Look at the labels to see which companies make these products. Unless you are completely different from most Americans, if these products and manufacturers are in your pantry, the chances are that they are in most of the pantries in the United States and, for that matter, the world. Start your list with the companies that make the products that you like the most. Now go into your bathroom. Check out the products you like the most in there and add the manufacturer to your list. What is your favorite toothpaste? Who makes the medicine in your medicine cabinet? The manufacturer is always listed on the label. Go to your living room. Who makes your TV? Which streaming services do you use on your TV? Which network channels do you watch? You may be surprised who owns the networks you watch. Do you have a cell phone? Of course. Which one? Which service provider do you use? Are you happy with it? Go to your garage. Who makes the tools on your workbench?

Who makes the cars you drive, and who makes the tires on the vehicles? For that matter, who makes the car you wish you could drive? Where do you buy the gas to fuel your car? Now, look inside your checkbook. Which bank do you use? Do you like it? Is it a big publicly traded bank? What companies do you write checks to regularly? Look at your credit card statements. Which cards do you use the most? Where do you use your card? Write down the names of all these businesses. Go to your office. Which computer do you use? Who makes the hardware inside it and the software on the computer? Write them down. If you think about it, how many publicly traded companies do you use regularly? Many people likely use the same companies. Shouldn't you invest in those companies and give yourself the potential to get some of your expenditure back in the form of profits or dividends? By the time you create that list, you're on your way to building your universe of stocks to watch.

This list is only limited by your imagination. Don't worry about whether you think it's a good or bad company. The reality is that you will figure that out as we go into the next phases of your analysis. You just need a list of companies with whom you are familiar and others that, for whatever reason, you have an interest in. Even though our universe is about 150 companies, you can probably get by with fewer. You might want to start out with 75, and you can adjust from there.

Chapter 4

Price to Earnings Ratio (P/E)

So, now you have your list of stocks to look at. We caution you, don't buy any yet! Wait for it, wait for it! Wait until you finish this book and see how every part of it builds on the next part to optimize your chances of building a great, elegant, logical, but easily understood portfolio. Now we start the real work. The first step is simple. Just look at your cell phone. Almost all newer model phones come with an app (like Yahoo Finance) that allows you to look up stocks and get their current prices (although some have a slight time delay of up to a few minutes), providing a fair amount of information useful for your investments. Later, as we review additional details of your analysis, you may want to consider subscribing to a more advanced research tool that offers more detailed analysis, although some of these tools may not be necessary. For the moment, though, let's look at the app on the phone.

You probably already know that each publicly traded stock has its own unique symbol. Most of these symbols are logical, and some are even humorously logical. For instance, Southwest Airlines, which is headquartered in Dallas and whose main hub is Love Field there, has the ticker symbol LUV, which has always seemed both logical and a little humorous. Six Flags Entertainment Corporation's symbol is FUN. Sports car manufacturer, Ferrari, has the symbol RACE. That seems appropriate if you don't know the symbol for the stock of a company you are considering, Google it.

When you have found your first stock symbol on your phone, a chart will usually appear on your phone screen. This will come in useful later. Under the chart, there will be a list of statistics about the company's vital financial numbers. The first thing we are interested in from that list is the most discussed, but least understood, of the company's vitals, items about a company that one may hear around the water cooler or at parties. The first item that we look at is the ratio between the price of the stock and the Earnings. This ratio is called the P/E ratio or simply PE, with the Price of the stock being the numerator and earnings per share over the last year being the denominator. This is probably the most discussed and least understood of a stock's vitals. Just as an explanation, if a stock has a market price of $100 and the total earnings per share for the previous 4 quarters are $10, the P/E would be 10 (100/10). The usual question here would be, is a PE of 10 a good ratio or a bad ratio? At the risk of sounding too lawyerly, the answer is, it depends. It depends on, for this book, whether the earnings are growing and how much the earnings are growing. But that is for the next chapter: Back to PE. The historical average PE of the stock market is 13 to 14, depending on the analyst. When the average PE goes above 17, you will hear the market analysts griping that the ratio is too high and the market is overvalued. Interestingly, the market can stay "overvalued" for several years at times. You should be able to see the P/E ratio on your phone when you look up a particular stock. Even though we don't know, at this point, whether the P/E is good or bad, we can learn a few things from it. The fact that a stock has a PE ratio indicates it has made a profit over the past 12 months. If they had lost money, that would have made the E in P/E a negative number, making the P/E impossible to calculate. A stock without a P/E ratio signals, in our minds, a potential problem. If you flip the numbers and make the price the denominator and the earnings the numerator, you get the earnings per price ratio or E/P. This tells you what kind of earnings you can theoretically expect to receive on each dollar you invest, assuming earnings stay constant in the future. Going back to our example above, this ratio would be shown as $10/$100 or 1/10. Expressed as a decimal, that would be .10 or 10%. Not a bad return on your investment. Remember, we said it is theoretical. This is because no earnings are guaranteed, and no price will remain completely stable. But if we assume a static market price and the future earnings prove to be the same, this would be the return that the company earns as a percentage of the stock price. Expanding on this, theoretically, if you owned the stock, you would expect your investment in the company to give you a 10% return on investment.

Your return on your investment needs to be defined here. Return on a stock would be dividends plus growth of the stock price. No company can pay out every dollar of its earnings as a dividend; some earnings must be retained in the company for future expenses and growth. So, our theoretical company may choose to pay shareholders a dividend of $2 per share and retain the remaining $ 8 in earnings. This would mean the assets of the company have grown by $8 per share, and the price of the stock may ultimately reflect that. Your return on the $100 per share investment would remain at 10%, comprising $2 in dividend payments from the company, plus a potential $8 of the profits left in the company's assets. Hopefully, the stock price will ultimately reflect this. Companies aren't required to pay dividends. Some choose to retain all of the earnings inside the assets of the company. That is fine if the company feels the total profits can be used to grow the company.

Besides the PE ratio making it possible to get an idea of the potential return on your investment, it also gives you an idea of how long it will take to break even on your investment. In this example, it would theoretically take you 10 years to see your investment break even ($100 investment divided by $10 in earnings per year would equal 10 years to break even). A PE of 20 would take 20 years, and a PE of 5 would take 5 years. Remember, these examples are assuming a static market and constant earnings.

We know we've been throwing a lot of numbers and ratios at you, and sometimes this can be a little (or very) boring. Still, this discussion is necessary to understand where we are going and for you to feel comfortable with your investment decisions. We are just trying to give you the tools to increase the potential of success. Therefore, if you didn't understand the previous discussion on the first reading, please go back and read it again...slowly. Just keep in mind that there are usually no guarantees when investing, and markets are not static. That is why we keep repeating the word "theoretically".

Chapter 5

The PEG Ratio

Now that we have a good understanding of Price to Earnings Ratios, we are ready to add one more layer to the strategy of finding great stocks in which to invest. As we discussed in the previous chapter, the P/E ratio can give you a reasonable idea of whether or not a stock is priced correctly in a static market (which rarely exists). Now, on a more realistic basis, most markets and stock prices are moving constantly, either up or down. Also, we can add another variable to the mix, the growth of projected earnings. Since we know that earnings per share of a stock are rarely static, we need to adjust our calculations to account for earnings growth or decline. Going back to our example of a stock with a market price of $100 per share and earnings per share of

$10. That stock would have a P/E of 10. Now, let's assume that the consensus of analysts who follow that stock has an average estimated earnings projection of $11 per share for next year. That would be an earnings growth of 10% ($11 for next year minus $10 for the previous year divided by $10 for last year). Would you be willing to pay more or less for a company that is expected to increase its earnings by 10% than you would for a company that will keep on earning a static $10 per share year after year? If you answered that you would pay more for the stock with the growing earnings, logically, that would be correct. That is, if the price is reasonable given the growth rate. So, how do we determine whether the price is reasonable, given the growth projections of earnings per share? There is a formula that is designed to help determine the answer to this question. It is called the PEG Rate. The formula is the price of the stock divided by the earnings per share of the stock divided by the projected annualized growth of earnings for a specific length of time, or P/E/G. In this example, the PEG rate is determined by dividing the stock price of $100 by the Earnings of 10 to get the PE of 10. Now divide that by the projected earnings growth of 10% (P/E/G). The PEG rate is 1. That means the earnings growth is equal to the PE. PEG Rates were first mentioned in Mario Farina's book, A Beginner's Guide to Successful Investing in the Stock Market, which was published in 1969. Since then, several analysts have used the ratio. The problem is that analysts are conflicted on several points:

1. What is the correct PEG rate that says a stock is a good price? Originally, Farina felt that a PEG rate of 1 (the growth of earnings was equal to the P/E ratio of the stock) indicated a buy. We will discuss this in more detail.

2. What period of time the growth rate should cover (originally, Farina used a 5-year annualized growth rate). Again, this will be covered later.
3. The term, growth, has been distorted from earnings growth to revenue growth and cash flow growth. We will give our preference.

Meanwhile, back to your phone. If you are using Yahoo Finance, click on the blue bar under the statistics below the chart. The blue line says More Data from Yahoo Finance. You will see a toolbar at the top of the page. Scroll to the left, and you will see the word Statistics as one of the options. Click on that. About 2/3 of the way down on the page that pops up, the PEG Ratio will appear. You can use that ratio to get a rough idea of the PEG. Notice, however, that it is a 5-year PEG, meaning they are using the 5-year growth rate, which is the average of the estimates of the analysts that follow the stock. We are skeptical that anyone can accurately predict a company's earnings 5 years out. We prefer to use earnings projections that are 1 year to 18 months out. They seem more accurate. To get those earnings projections, you will most likely need to subscribe to an expensive outside source or ask your financial advisor to help you. Financial advisors are valuable tools that we will discuss later. We also try to use only stocks that several analysts cover to get an average of the earnings estimates. If only one analyst follows the stock, you will be subject to his/her biases about the company, right or wrong. We find that a larger universe of analysts following a stock gives a more accurate earnings projection.

I was originally introduced to PEG rates by a friend of mine from my church over lunch one day. He was the CFO of a Fortune 500 company. I was a young, new stockbroker, eager to learn. His company was profitable, and the analysts felt that the company's earnings would grow over the next 5 years at a rate equal to the P/E. It had a PEG rate of 1, and he said that some analysts had recommended the stock based on the PEG rate. I was intrigued and watched the stock instead of buying it, since I was a new broker and had never heard of PEG rates. To my surprise, delight, and envy, the stock began to rise in price shortly after this meeting. Obviously, this sparked my interest in both the stock and PEG rates as an arrow in my quiver of parameters with which to pick good stocks. I began to investigate the PEG rates of several stocks. It was not easy, at the time, to find stocks that had a PEG rate of 1. Many stocks with earnings had no projected INCREASE in earnings. However, there were a few nuggets to be found, and those seemed to work. But more interesting was the fact that there were still stocks, with PEG rates greater than 1, that seemed to move up in price. Why was that? The most common factor among these stocks was their growth in earnings, which was projected to continue into the future. So, in my young, feeble mind, I decided that a PEG rate of 1 shouldn't be the determining factor as long as the earnings were growing and the stock price was moving up. I was always looking for an opportunity to learn. By the way, I don't like the word opportunity. When I first graduated from college, I went to work for Procter & Gamble, the giant consumer products company. A great company with excellent training. The first time my boss called me and said we had an opportunity, I was excited. Opportunities are supposed to be good, right? I quickly learned that in business speak, "opportunity" means "you messed something up and now you have to fix it" or "you're getting ready to learn a lesson the hard way". But I digress, back to my "opportunity "to learn about PEG rates. I decided to begin investing in stocks that had growing earnings. I started buying a large and great software company, with earnings growing steadily. I calculated the PEG rate when I started buying. It had a PEG rate of 2 as I made my first purchases for clients. The stock price continued to rise, and earnings were growing. I bought some more for clients. The PEG was up to 3 by then. It went up some more. I thought I'd figured this thing out. You buy a stock with growing earnings, and its price will climb. And then, the lesson began. Suddenly, the stock price quit growing. Then it started dropping. "Don't investors understand that as long as earnings are growing, the stock will go up in price", I said to myself. Wrong! It turns out that there is an upper limit to what an investor will pay for a stock. As I tried to find the reason for the stock to put on its proverbial brakes, I did some new calculations. The PEG rate, it turns out, was now 6, not 2 as it was when I started buying. Interestingly, the stock price had grown faster than earnings growth by a significant amount. That led to a substantial rise in the PEG rate. I began looking at other stocks. I soon realized that a few stocks could continue growing in price for an extended amount of time with PEG rates that high. So, what is the lesson I had "the opportunity" to learn? The stock moved up fine with a PEG rate of 2 and even 3, but it stopped increasing in price when the PEG was 6. Therefore, to me, it seemed that the ideal PEG rate at which to buy a stock is somewhere below 6, but can be greater than 2.

-Roy

Through years of trial and error, we have found that our ideal comfortable PEG rate at which to buy a stock is anything less than or equal to 3; the closer to a PEG rate of 1, the better. At times, we have found great stocks with PEG rates below 1, but those are few and far between. We will not buy a stock with a PEG over 3. We will, however, happily, let the PEG increase after we already own it until we feel the stock is getting tired and overpriced. We will discuss when to sell stocks in a later chapter. It is necessary to warn you that finding a stock with a PEG under 3 is not the total reason to start buying it. The great thing about using PEG rates as our primary source of fundamental analysis is that it combines the past, present, and future. The past comes from the trailing 12-month earnings (E), the present comes from the current price of the stock (P), and the future comes from the analysts' average estimate of the next one or two years' earnings (G). By the way, the more analysts the better. The average of a greater # of analysts seems to be more accurate.

Let's look at a real example. XYZ is selling at $499 per share. It has made $13.64 per share over the last 12 months. That would give it a P/E of 36.48. Using our advanced stock service, I can see that the average of the 60 analysts that follow XYZ projects the earnings in the fiscal year ending in June of 2027 to be 18.27. Now we need to find the growth rate of earnings that are projected between now and then. First, we find the overall growth rate, which is 18.27 (fiscal earnings for 2027)- 13.64(trailing 12 months earnings)/13.64 (trailing 12 months earnings.) That will give us the overall growth rate for the period of 33.94%. To find the annualized growth rate, divide the growth rate by the # of years of the projection. Assume our current month is August 2025. This formula would be 33.94/1.833 (years) = 18.5 annualized growth rate. Now, in order to find the PEG, divide the PE by the growth rate. 36.48/18.55= 1.966. That falls well within our maximum acceptable PEG of 3. So, if other factors discussed in the following chapters were in line, the tech company might have been a buy on this date.

This is obviously not a recommendation to take any action on that company as you read this book. Just an exercise in a real-life example.

As mentioned above, the PEG on your phone's financial pages usually gives a 5-year annualized projected earnings growth and corresponding PEG. We feel that earnings growth over the next one to two years tends to be more accurate. To get this kind of estimate, you will need a more advanced stock search program (or your financial advisor) than the phone provides. There are several stock research services available. Not only are their estimates more usable, but they also come with stock charts that can be tweaked to suit your use.

Below is a short list of stock research companies that we have used or of which we are aware:

1. Morningstar
2. FactSet
3. Kwant
4. Quodd
5. Thomson Reuters
6. Y Charts

These services will charge for the subscription, so don't be surprised and don't order one until you finish this book. You might not need to. We will add the final layer to our buying parameters in the next chapter. Don't start buying yet.

Chapter 6

Charts- What Do Emotions Look Like?

The final parameter that we look at before buying a stock is that stock's chart, that mystical, magical, much maligned but often misunderstood picture of a stock's action over time. This is perhaps the most difficult part of our buying equation to understand because it can be very subjective. Our goal is to try to eliminate as much of the subjectivity as possible and break the technical analysis down to an easily followed process. Fundamental investors (those who use strictly the mathematical tools to determine whether to buy a stock) commonly don't like to use charts. We have heard it described as voodoo forecasting. More realistic is the fact that, for the most part, charts can't be interpreted by the hard and fast mathematics that fundamental analysis uses. Charting, commonly known as technical analysis, takes an experienced eye with some creativity. We feel that technical analysis must be used in conjunction with fundamental analysis to try to determine a good point to start buying a quality stock that passes our previous fundamental analysis. Keep in mind, though, that even with great fundamental and technical analysis, accuracy can't be guaranteed. If you have trouble believing that, just watch CNBC for a few days. Virtually all the "expert," analysts will readily admit that sometimes stocks and the markets don't act in the manner they anticipated.

When I was a young broker, our office held a large client meeting at which our firm's Chief Technical Analyst would speak. This was a really big deal. He was nationally known and was frequently a guest on CNBC and other business networks. The day of the meeting, I was asked to drive the analyst to several TV stations with which he had interviews scheduled. As a curious young broker, aware of the fact that I had such a well-known expert as a captive source of information, I asked him, "What is the most important thing a financial advisor needs to do to be successful?" He calmly looked at me and said, in the deep voice of a college professor, "Roy, what one needs to be successful as an advisor is to have a degree in Psychology and a Master's in Abnormal Psychology."

-Roy

Even with that warning, we have found, however, that using the combination of fundamental and technical analysis has increased our performance, improved our likelihood of successful recommendations in the short run, and reduced our less-than-accurate recommendations.

A stock's chart is simply the stock price marked on a graph over a specific period of time. It is a snapshot of investor emotions. During that period, you will see the stock price rise and fall. We feel that these price movements, in their simplest forms, are a time-lapse moving picture of investor emotions. It can be described as an emotional EKG. As the chart moves up, this means that more investors have seen something they like or anticipate and are more interested in buying the stock rather than selling it. Conversely, if the chart is moving down, more investors have seen something concerning to them. Remember, just because a stock has a chart that is moving downward at a given time doesn't necessarily mean it is a bad company. It's just not the right time to buy the stock. If you have done your homework and have gone through the fundamental exercises and the stock has a good PEG rate, all you must do is wait for the charts to tell you when emotions have turned and to start buying again.

Below are the rules that we use to determine when to begin buying.

1. Take a look at your list of companies that you put together in Chapter 1. This is your universe of stocks to watch. We go through our list every day. You might want to do this daily, or go through it once a week or month. You want to keep your stock universe large enough to have a wide mix of industries and company sizes, but small enough that the time you spend going through it does not become so cumbersome that it keeps you from other things necessary in your life. It depends on

how active you want to be. We recommend going through your universe of stocks at least once a week.

2. Assuming you have done your fundamental analysis on your universe of stocks, you will have found some that pass those parameters and have good, workable PEG rates. Look at the charts of these qualifying companies. These are the companies whose charts you want to study for that day. Each time you do your fundamental homework, you will see that some stocks are the same as your previous filter, but usually, there will also be some new ones that show up as buys.

3. The first objective in the current analysis period is to eliminate companies within 10% of the stock's high over the past 52 weeks. They are likely to be good companies, but are not buyable in this analysis period. The reason for this is that we don't want to buy a stock unless we think it will have a chance of at least reaching the level of its 52-week high again over the next year. We want to feel that we have a high probability of achieving at least a 10% return if it does that. By only buying stocks that are selling at less than 90% of the 52-week highs, if they go back to these highs, we have achieved at least the minimum 10% return. Obviously, we would like it to go to new highs and beyond, if possible, but giving the stock at least a 10% runway can give us a nice return if it just gets back to the highs.

4. The fourth technical parameter we look for is an upward trend. Don't get too excited if a stock you like seems to shoot up one day. Keep in mind one of our primary rules. We have said it over and over again to clients and new brokers. It is a simple rule. ONE DAY DOES NOT A TREND MAKE! We even have to remind ourselves of this rule from time to time. We started looking for three up days in a row as our definition for the beginning of a trend. We finally expanded our parameters to look for 3 of the last 4 days to be up, including the day we are looking at the chart. Ideally, those 3 out of 4 days need to go higher than the price on the day before that trend started. This discipline has reduced our chances of moving into stocks too early and helped our clients grow their assets over the years.

There are several patterns that stocks make as they go up and down, for which black belt technical analysts look. There are several good books that describe these patterns if you want to study them in more depth. These books are also good when you can't sleep, and you need something to help you catch some z's. Our philosophy is that when you study these patterns, you will find that they all start with at least 3 up days, or 3 out of 4 up days. We feel that this is a good trend to look for, and using this rule has helped us tremendously.

All charts in this book are taken from actual stocks during the time period mentioned. The names and symbols of these stocks have been changed to protect the innocent.

Take a look at chart 1 on page 49. This is a one-year chart of stock ABC. The chart begins in March of 2024. What is not seen on the chart is that the prior 52-week trading high was 154, set on January 29th. Per our rules, we would not want to buy the stock if it is within 90% of this 52-week high. The maximum buying price is 138 (154 x .9). We are looking for 3 out of 4 up days. This occurred on March 11th when the stock was trading at 137.50. This buy is marked with the number one. The PEG rate of 1 was in our buying range. We realize that the price of the stock on 3/11 was only half a point under the 138 maximum buying price, but it was a buy just the same. As it happens, the stock closed above 138 on the 12th (#2). This first buying date was very fortuitous since the stock ran for the next 4 months all the way up to 191.18 on July 11 (#3), at which time it began a pullback. Since the PEG was still only a little over 1 at that time; it would not create a sell rating. Just wait, sit on the profits, and wait for the next 3 out of 4 up days to buy another tranche of the stock.

This second buying opportunity occurred on August 13th (#4) when the stock hit 164. Notice that the new 52-week high is now 191.18 (#3) from July 11th, and the maximum buying price would be 90% of that at 172.06 (191.18 x .9). Another buying date was on 8/20 (#5) at 167. At that point, it began slipping back again. Since the PEG was still around 1, the fundamentals were still in place, so we waited for our next buying trigger, which occurred on 9/13 (#6) when it hit

146. An item of note is that we try to buy equal dollar amounts of the stock (not equal share amounts). This tends to force an averaging down of the stock price since the same dollar amount would buy more shares at lower prices and fewer shares at higher prices. To prove this, we hypothetically bought four equal dollar positions of GOOG. If we assume we bought approximately $5,000 each time, this would give us the following:

First purchase: 36 shares at 138.94, total dollar amount of $5001.84.

Second purchase 30 shares at 165.39, total dollar amount $4961.7.

Third purchase 30 shares at 168.4, total dollar amount of $5052.

Fourth purchase 32 shares @155.54, total $amount of $4972.

The average share price is 156.19. At the end point of this chart, our purchases (cost basis) averaged over 9 points below the closing price of the Software Company on October 21st, even though the third purchase was made $2.80 higher than the end point price. If, on the other hand, we had purchased an equal number of shares each time, our average cost would have been $157.05 per share. We will refer to this chart throughout the book.

Chart 1

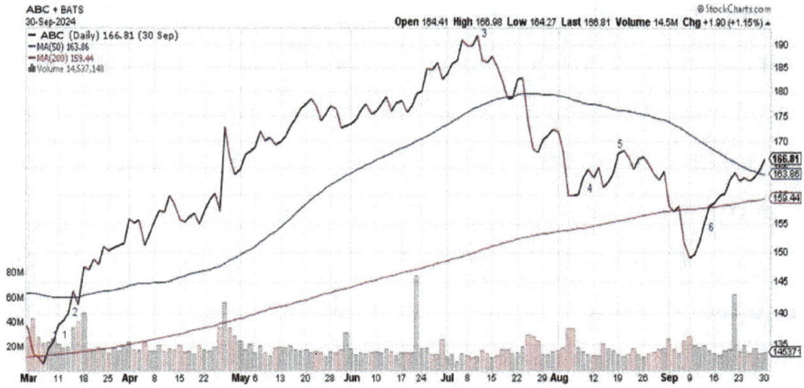

1. *First 3 out of 4 up days, buy at $138.94 per share.*
2. *Last buy opportunity at 90% of the previous 52-week high (which was $154.84) will be at $139.00 per share.*
3. *New 52-week high at $193.31. Ninety percent is $173.98.*
4. *First 3 out of 4 up days, buy at $165.39 per share.*
5. *Buy at $168.40.*
6. *Buy at $155.54.*

Next, you will want to set your charts. You cannot do this on your phone, Yahoo Finance. If you subscribe to one of the research and chart services, you can set several parameters. Set the charts to show the 50-day and 200-day moving averages of stocks. These averages are important to watch. Technical analysts almost universally use these averages. They are basically the mean average of the emotions of investors in the stock during that period. They seem almost to have magical, mystical powers. Often, as the stock moves up, it will hit one of these averages. Sometimes the stock will bounce down, at least temporarily, after it hits that point. Other times, it will blast through that average and begin moving up at a faster rate over the following days. The 50-day and 200-day averages are also important to watch for another reason. Let's say that a stock has a 200-day moving average at one level and the 50- day at a higher level. If the stock begins to drop and the 50-day moving average moves down to and through the 200-day average, that can be a sell signal for the stock. Some analysts call this a Death Cross. It means that the near-term stock action is going down faster and can pull the stock price even lower. The emotions of the investors are getting more and more negative. The opposite can be true if the 50-day blows through the 200-day on the way up. That's a bullish sign. But we digress. Just be aware of these averages and watch the stock's historic action as it meets them. The lesson in this discussion is to keep an eye open for stocks that are up at least 3 of the last 4 days. If, however, the stock goes up to within a dollar of its 50 or 200-day moving average, stop buying temporarily. Wait to see if it goes through that average or bounces back down once it touches it. If it bounces down, just wait for it to head back up and reload the last 3 days of the 4-day rule. When the stock finally does break through the average lines, it can be seen as a buy again, even if the 3-out-of-4-day rule hasn't been achieved yet. Refer again to the ABC Chart 1. Notice that on March 7, 2024, it bounced off the 200-day moving average.

This coincidentally was the first day of the 3 out of 4 up days required to create a buy on the stock. Also, on the way up, on March 17th, it hit the 50-day moving average and pulled back for a day before blowing through that average and going to new highs. And, on the way down (July 20th), it bounced off that average for a few days before breaking through (July 25th), and it was on its way down.

As well as the 50- and 200-day averages, keep an eye on the most recent near-term peaks in a stock's chart. We're not talking about all-time highs or even 52-week highs here, just the most recent peaks before the stock started pulling back. At times, that can be a warning level, and the stock may at least temporarily pull back once it hits that point again. The logic to this is that at the point the original peak was made, some investors bought the stock at that price, thinking it would go higher immediately. When it started moving down after they bought, they became disgruntled investors, and some lost confidence in themselves and the stock. They promise themselves that they will sell as soon as it gets back to the price they paid for the stock, so at least they will be even. This puts some selling pressure on the stock as it touches the previous near-term peak. If there are enough of these investors who want out, the stock can pull back as they sell. It will continue this short-term up and down pattern until the worries are out of the stock, allowing it to pop through the previous peak. Then the remaining previous buyers begin feeling better about themselves and the little profits they are making, and will hang on to it to enjoy the ride up or even buy more as it breaks out and moves up to the next peak, and the process repeats. These reactions are emotional investing and not recommended. Observe this action several times in XYZ's chart, specifically between April 13th and May 1st, and between May 20th and June 18th. Suffice it to say, when a stock moves past a recent peak, it may become a buy if the other parameters are in place. Hopefully, that coincides with the 3-out-of-4-day rule. If not, crossing the previous peak overrides the 3 out of 4 up days rule.

Look at PQR's trading patterns on Chart 2 on page 55. Observe that it peaked in May of 2023, then fell sharply until it hit its 200-day moving average at the end of that month. It immediately started moving higher until August, when it touched roughly the same level as the earlier peak. At that point, some of the investors who had bought at the previous peak were at breakeven and were just happy to get their original investment back after the drop. They began selling. Some of the investors who had bought at the bottom of the trough or on the way back up decided they had a decent profit and, after seeing the start of another downturn, took their gains (In other words, they sold). So, the downturn began again, and the process repeated itself two more times (troughs B and C) before the stock went up through the original peak, and a breakout began. Note that each trough was slightly higher than the previous one, and there were several buying opportunities for long-term investors to buy. These short-term pullbacks created a pattern of higher highs and higher lows. Look for these patterns. They are positive. Also note that the breakout occurred almost simultaneously to the point where the 50-day average moved above the 200-day average in late January. This is almost a textbook chart.

If the chart service you use has a way to show a chart of the daily volume of shares traded on a stock, set it up and use it in conjunction with the price movements. Volume seems to pick up as a stock is beginning to break out to new, higher levels. Whereas we don't think the volume is the deciding factor on whether to buy a stock, it can give you some comfort as you buy if the volume is rising. This means that other investors are starting to see the same positive signs as you, or they see other reasons and are acting on them by purchasing the stock.

This is why we say that a stock's chart is just a moving picture of investor emotions. The famous investor Warren Buffett said, "Be fearful when others are greedy and greedy when others are fearful." Troughs represent fearful investors. The motions, and peaks represent greedy investor emotions. Buy a little when others are fearful, assuming the stock meets e other buying parameters.

Chart 2

PQR NYSE + BATS
28-Feb-2024
@StockCharts.com
Open 154.28 High 155.30 Low 153.86 Last 155.23 Volume 3.9M Chg +0.73 (+0.47%)
PQR(Daily) 155.23 (28 Feb)
MA(50) 147.84
MA(200) 144.91
Volume 3,920,984
Peak
Retracement
Breakout
A
B
C
155.23
154
152
150
147.84
146
144.91
144
142
140
138
136
134
132
25M
20M
15M
10M
5M
Mar
Apr
May
Jun
Jul
Aug
Sep
Oct
Nov
Dec
2024
Feb

Every time I discuss the above process, I am reminded of the time when my youngest son, Will, got a Pogo Stick for Christmas. My sons, Ryan, Travis, and Will, being the young rambunctious kids that they were, became tired of jumping on the Pogo Stick outdoors. "What's the challenge in that?" they asked. Almost immediately, they brought it inside the house and began jumping on it on the tile floor of the kitchen. I asked them why they were doing that, and they said that they were trying to see if they could jump high enough to touch the ceiling with the top of their head. Amazingly, as they practiced, it turned out that they could just barely touch it. As they practiced more, they hit it more and more often and harder and harder. I have sometimes wondered if that ceiling bashing with their heads might have been responsible for some of the less-than-wise things that they did at times in their teen years. Also, don't worry, there was no structural damage to the house after this happened. Soon, they grew tired of hitting their head on the ceiling. One of them turned and looked at the staircase that went up to the second floor. They all locked eyes with each other as sly grins formed on their collective faces. Suddenly, they moved in mass toward the staircase with the Pogo Stick. I was a kid once and knew exactly what they were thinking. The thought sounded fun in my brain, but the thought of yet another trip to the emergency room and explaining the injury to the doctor sounded like no fun to me. Before the first son could begin jumping on the first step of the staircase, I grabbed the stick and dragged it outside with all three dragging behind it. "No more Pogo Sticks in the house". "Ah, Dad".

Now let's assume I hadn't commandeered the Pogo Stick, and the boys had used it to hop merrily up the stairs to the second floor without breaking any bones, sconces, or other decorations in the house. Once they hit the top step, they would have explored the top floor of our humble abode before attempting to go back down the stairs. That thought was really terrifying. Now here is the visual. If you look at the top of my son's head as points on a stock chart, you will see that when he was downstairs and bashing his head against the ceiling, the same action occurs that a stock makes as it goes up and down before it starts moving to higher levels. This is the ceiling or high of the current stock action. As he started up the stairs, his head was unobstructed, and suddenly it was higher than the downstairs ceiling. He has broken through the previous high. Once he gets to the top of the stairs, the downstairs ceiling now becomes the floor on the second level. Often, stocks move in a similar manner when they finally break through previous highs. Now, those previous highs act as a new floor or base. In the Pogo Stick example, the ceiling on the second floor now becomes a new barrier. If the house had three levels, he would have had to bounce around until he found the new staircase up again. There is one more point to make, a still another visual. As he moved up the steps, his head would have gone up and down, but each step would have been higher than the previous one, followed by a slight drop as he came down to the next step. This makes a series of higher highs and higher lows as he makes it up the stairs. This is the action of a normal stock chart as the stock seeks its higher level, higher highs, and higher lows.

-Roy

Yet one more visual, as we kick a dead horse, the action, as the stock goes up, is like watching a kid with a yo-yo as he goes upstairs. Each high is higher than the previous high, and each low is higher than the previous low. This is a pattern you want to see.

At some point, the stock may get to new highs where there are no investors who have bought at a higher level. Therefore, very little selling pressures are seen. We have found that once stocks make it to new long-term highs, if they are meeting our fundamental parameters, the average return from that point has been about 26% before profit takers start moving out of their positions. That is not a guarantee, just our observations over many years and many stocks. Some investors wait until a stock reaches these lofty levels before they begin buying. Their strategy is to buy high and sell higher. We feel that a stock becomes riskier the higher it gets, so we stick to our strategy of buying low and selling high. In baseball terms, we will hit a lot of singles and doubles and cash in on those gains. Occasionally, some of those turn into home runs. A great investor, Shelby Davis, who founded the Davis Funds, said, "You make most of your money in a bear market, you just don't realize it at the time." He meant that you should catch stocks close to the lows and hold them to optimum profitability. A friend in the used car business told Roy that most of the profit comes from the buy. If you buy at a low price, you stand a much better chance of making a profit, and you don't have to sell the car at an unreasonably high price to do it. Those who buy at high prices can leave a lot of potential profits on the side while they wait for the stock to reach their desired price and then hope the stock will go higher. Now, you should be able to see how charts are a picture of investor emotions and psychology and are a viable part of your investment strategy. Just a word to those who will listen, hope is not a strategy.

We have now discussed the important parameters you should use to determine which stocks to buy and when to start buying. Remember, fundamental analysis allows you to find the stocks in your universe to buy. Technical analysis gives you a relatively reliable strategy for determining when to buy them. Even when all the above are put into practice, though, there are no guarantees of success. We have found, however, that following this strategy does lessen the number of bad calls, increases investment performance, and gives confidence in making the buying decisions.

Chapter 7

How to buy

It is one thing to know which stocks to buy and when to buy them; it is another thing to understand how to buy.

In the popular TV game show, Jeopardy, one very successful contestant was a professional sports gambler named James Holzhauer. He is the third highest American game show winner to date and went on to win the Tournament of Champions. His trademark on the show was, when he would hit a daily double question in a category in which he felt comfortable, pushing his hands forward and saying “all in” as though he was pushing his whole pot of chips in while playing poker.

We have a hard and fast rule: IT IS NEVER ALL IN AND IS RARELY ALL OUT. Our experience is that investors, once they find what they think is a good stock, tend to get overly excited about it. They want to put in everything that they have allocated to that position all at once. Instead, our strategy is to put a portion (usually about 20%) of the money allocated to an investment into it to open the position and then watch it carefully. If it continues to go up in price and the parameters are still in place, add the same amount of dollars with which you opened the position. Repeat this pattern until you have invested the entire allocation toward that stock position. For example, if you have $10,000 to add a new stock to your diversified portfolio, begin buying that stock with a $2,000 purchase. When the next buy signal occurs, add another $2,000 and so on until the full $10,000 is invested in the stock. Note, a lot of times, the next buy signal is the next day after the first trade. If it goes down but still meets the parameters of a good buy, let it. Don't panic and sell out. Fundamentally, it is still a buyable stock. Go back to the technical analysis and wait for it to be up 3 out of 4 days or cross over a strategic point and buy more shares in the same dollar amount as the first purchase with the second allocation. Continue the process until the entire allocation is purchased. At this point, you may want to review the chart 1 of ABC and reread the analysis of it.

The logic of this buying strategy is that if you are buying roughly equal dollars of the stock each time you purchase. You will buy more shares with the same dollar amount at lower prices and fewer shares at a time of higher prices. This discipline tends to average your cost lower, as we have seen in the ABC chart explanation. Also, remember that it is fine to buy shares at higher prices than your initial purchase if the stock still meets our buying parameters. The advantage of doing this is that the stock has moved up from the initial purchase, which means you have likely caught it on a bull move, increasing the potential for gains.

As you continue to buy in the same dollar increments while it is rising, you will be buying slightly fewer shares at higher prices. So, suppose the stock maintains its buying parameters. In that case, there are advantages to adding to your initial position, whether it is higher or lower at the time of the add-on purchases. This strategy is called dollar cost averaging. This is the same strategy that most portfolio managers use. This strategy helps you control your emotions when you buy. A lot of people get so excited about an attractive stock that they put the entire allocation into one large purchase. We believe this is usually the wrong strategy and is an emotional buy. Benjamin Graham, one of Warren Buffett's mentors, said, "Individuals who cannot master their emotions are ill-suited to profit from the investment process.".

The major points of the above discussion are:

1) Don't buy your entire position in one shot. It is never all in at once.

2) Divide the total position you are willing to own into several tranches and buy equal dollar amounts for each tranche as the stock moves up or down, if it still meets our investment parameters.

3) Don't talk yourself out of buying the next tranche if the stock pulls back, as long as the buying parameters are still there. Just wait for the 3-out-of-4-day rule to materialize.

4) Don't panic and sell out if the buying parameters are still in place.

Now you own the stock. What now?

Enjoy the ride. Let it run until the parameters aren't there.

Chapter 8

When to sell

Let's assume you bought your entire allocated position in a stock over several tranches. You have held the stock for a while. At what point do you sell it to take your profits or cut your losses. Remember, even when they meet the best parameters, not all stocks go up forever. There are myriad reasons why they begin a downturn. But sometimes you just need to get out of a stock or at least lighten up on your position.

We believe one of the most obvious times to start selling a stock is when a mirror image of the buying process begins to appear. The stock has reached its highs, the fundamental parameters are not there anymore, and the PEG rate has gone above 3. The stock has been down for 3 out of the past 4 trading days and trades below its most recent low. Ideally, that is the perfect sell signal. But, as in everything else stock-related, such a clear sell is rarely seen.

As a stock begins to climb, most of the time there is an (to quote my American History teachers) "Era of Good Feeling" that often leads to Euphoria. You feel like you can make no mistakes, and you have the next great stock that will make you millions. You may tend to fall in love with the stock or have strong emotional ties to it. We have 7 words for you, **don't fall in love with your stocks!** Be in love with your spouse, not your stock.

Eventually, you may have to sell all or part of your favorite stock, and it's better not to be emotionally attached. We have had clients who have fallen in love with a stock. It forces them to make irrational emotional decisions instead of rational financial decisions. When we see a client exhibiting signs of "stock love" and point it out to them, they invariably say that they aren't. But the proof is whether they can cut the ties with the stock and sell it at the right time. The common rationalizations are "it will come back," or "It will go higher," or "the analysts don't realize that (choose your excuse)." Of course, the same thing can happen with irrational stock hate. You have been burned in a stock several times, and it seems like there is nothing that can make you buy it again, even if the buy parameters are all there. We call either of these emotional situations "creative irrationality." You must keep reminding yourself that second-rate stocks can be great buys at the right price and great companies can be terrible buys or holds at the wrong prices. We now refer you back to Benjamin Graham's quote, "Individuals who cannot master their emotions are ill-suited to profit from the investment process."

It is much easier to decide when to buy a stock than to determine when to sell it. No one enjoys admitting they made a mistake when they bought the stock if it is down. Conversely, it is difficult to sell a stock when it is up. Part of the reason is that once you sell the stock, to keep your money working for you, you must find another alternative to replace it and hope that it will go up. All investors have this conflict in their minds, including us and every other financial advisor or asset manager. This mental debate is one of the reasons that we say, "It's never all in and rarely all out." Just as when you buy, we recommend breaking the purchase into a series of tranches; we also recommend selling the stock incrementally. We usually sell about a quarter of the shares at a time. Notice that this is a higher incremental percentage of the position than you purchased the stock. Also, we sell a percentage of the total number of shares, not the total dollar amount. This process will get you out of more dollars at a higher price as the stock moves down. The reason for this is that stocks seem to fall faster than they go up. An old axiom is that "stocks take an escalator up and an elevator down." If you are selling under ideal situations (the stock has run up to within 10% of the 52-week highs or higher and seems to have topped out, and the buying parameters are slipping), you should be selling with a decent profit. Since you would have bought it at a lower price using the buying rules, sell a quarter of the shares. It is good to lock in a portion of the profit. If the assumption that it isn't going higher is wrong and the stock continues to climb, great, you will continue to participate with three-quarters of the original position. If, however, it does decline, you have locked in some profit, and you can sell more. Remember, it is rarely wrong to lock in some of the profits. If, after the second sell, the stock meets the rest of the parameters, but the chart is still moving down, you might want to wait before you sell a third tranche. A lot of times, a stock will take a short-term breather and pull back before loading up the spring in the pogo stick and taking off again. Review the chart 2 of PQR again. The stock pulled back several times from peaks. Those pullbacks created opportunities. Coming off the troughs at points A, B, and C created great buying opportunities. If the parameters are still there and the price is below 90% of its 52-week high mark, you can always buy more after 3 out of the past 4 trading days are up for the stock, according to the buying rules.

Let's say that a stock has been a buy, but you see that the analysts have recently lowered their projected earnings' estimates and the stock no longer meets our fundamental parameters (such as a PEG rate that has exceeded 3), we usually begin the selling process regardless of where the stock is in its range. Sometimes this means we may be selling at a loss.

I remember when I was a young advisor, I heard my manager ask a client, "Now let me get this straight, do you want more money or less money?" He felt that a stock should be sold because of lowered earnings estimates, and the client wanted to hang on to it instead of selling. It seemed obvious to the manager that the stock was going lower. A partial sell at the time of the call could have placated both parties.

-Roy

Just remember the elevator analogy, they go down fast. Sometimes, if the parameters aren't there, you might want to move out of the position entirely. Your choice then is to increase the proportion of your position to sell, or sell the tranches on successive days, with the goal of getting out of the entire position. A lot of times, the stock will have a bounce after dropping for a few days, giving you the opportunity to get out of a tranche at a slightly higher level.

The most frustrating event we have encountered is that, after a position is sold, the stock starts moving up for no apparent reason. That phenomenon is called being whipsawed. It happens to everyone from time to time. It doesn't mean you made the wrong decision to sell if the parameters for continued ownership just weren't there.

Another source of frustration is if the analysts raise their earnings estimate right after you sell, and the stock becomes a roaring buy again. These things happen. You're not clairvoyant, and neither you nor your advisor has a crystal ball. You must just accept it and go on as though it is a new stock. Evaluate the situation and decide whether you should begin buying again. For these reasons, using the tranche method of selling a stock seems to work better than just selling the entire position at once.

Go to Chart 3 on page 72. You will see a chart of 123. As the stock came off its highs in April of 2004, the PEG was over 2. A high stock with a PEG above 2 needs to be watched closely, but still allowed some leeway as it floats around. At the point that it crossed below its 50-day moving average on 4/17, we began selling the first tranche (25% of the shares). It rallied for a few days but hit the 50-day average and reversed down on April 26 before heading back down. That triggered a second sell. Once again, it rallied before turning down and crossing below the 50-day average on 5/6. This action created the third sell trigger. From that point, it fell below the 90% mark of the previous high and, since it had a PEG below 3, would have had a Pass rating (not a buy or sell). On June 28th, it crossed below the 200-day moving average. That triggered a fourth sell. We were virtually out of the stock at that point. It finally bottomed on 8/13. On 8/16, it completed 3 consecutive up days. We look for 3 out of 4 up days with a PEG under 3 and the stock trading below 90% of its 52-week highs. This triggered a buy. At the time of this writing, it continues to be in an upward trend, and there have been several potential buy days. It is within a dollar of the 50-day moving average, so we pause while we anxiously wait to see if it goes through that line. If so, we will buy another tranche.

Chart 3

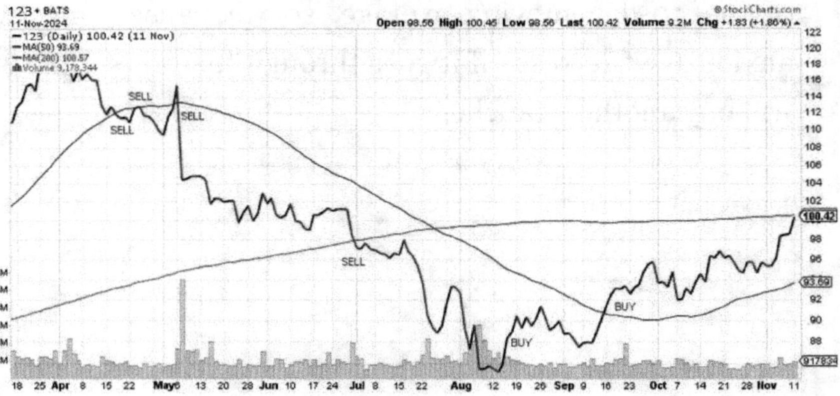

123 • BATS
11-Nov-2024
©StockCharts.com
Open 98.56 High 100.46 Low 98.56 Last 100.42 Volume 9.2M Chg +1.83 (+1.86%)
—123 (Daily) 100.42 (11 Nov)
—MA(50) 93.69
—MA(200) 100.57
Volume 9,178,344
SELL
SELL
SELL
SELL
BUY
BUY
100.42
93.69
18 25 Apr 8 15 22 May 6 13 20 28 Jun 10 17 24 Jul 8 15 22 Aug 12 19 26 Sep 9 16 23 Oct 7 14 21 28 Nov 11

Chapter 9

Trailing Stop Orders

One of the best tools for selling that we have found is trailing stop orders. This type of order works well if you are thinking of taking some profits on a stock because it has had a great run or the investment parameters are no longer in place, but you feel that there is a chance that it may go even higher. On the other hand, you don't want to lose all your profits if it begins pulling back. The trailing stop order is an excellent tool for this dilemma. A trailing stop order allows you to enter an order to sell a stock if the price pulls back to a point below which you don't feel comfortable holding the entire position. It gives you a chance to bank some profits or minimize losses. It is expressed as a percentage pullback of the existing price. If the stock pulls back by that percent, it will become a market sell order. You don't have to sell your entire position with this order. Going back to the previous discussion, logically, you would want to enter the trailing stop order to sell 25% of the position. Let's consider this situation. You have been able to accumulate 200 shares of XYZ stock following our guidelines. You now have a 25% profit. The stock has run up to within 10% of the 52-week high, and now the PEG rate has gone above 3, either because of appreciation or the analysts lowering next year's earnings estimates. The stock continues to move up in price. Do you sell now and take your profits? If you do, the stock may continue to climb. If it does, will it hurt your ego to miss out on the potential extra gain? You are a busy person and can't watch the market constantly. If you don't sell part of it now, you may not be able to catch the stock as it peaks before turning down. The best tool that we have found to solve this problem is the trailing stop order. The trailing stop order should be looked at as a form of insurance on the part of your position on which you place the order. The deductible on that insurance is paid when you sell it. And there is no charge (or premium in insurance terms) when you put in the order, although there may be a commission when it executes. You can put in an order to sell 25 percent of the shares of your total position in the stock if it pulls back 7% from any high point after the order is placed. The stock can continue to run, but if it pulls back from whichever point it rises by 7% it will execute. In insurance terms, that 7% would be equivalent to your deductible for the protection against further loss on that part of your position. Remember, the main reason for the existence of insurance is risk management. You buy life insurance on your life to help your beneficiaries deal with the risk of loss of your income. You buy homeowner's insurance to help you deal with the risk of losing your home in a fire or storm, and you buy car insurance to help you cover the risk of losing your car or financial risk in a wreck. Why not consider taking out insurance to help manage the risk of loss on a profitable portfolio?

Since you were up 25% on your position when you entered the order, you now have locked in an 18% profit (25%- 7%) on those shares. If the stock drops by 7% after entering the order, the order will be executed. If, however, it rises after you place your trailing stop order, the order will increase with the stock price. The order will continue to rise if the stock is rising. If at any time, the stock pulls back by 7 percent from the amount to which it has increased, it will execute. If the stock continues to drop but still meets the fundamental buying parameters, you can sell more, put in another trailing stop order (if you choose this option, we would recommend a 5% stop on the second tranche), or just wait for the stock to stop dropping. You know it is a good company and, eventually, since it still meets the fundamental buying parameters, in theory, it should stop dropping and begin its climb again at some point. At that time, if it still matches the fundamental buying rules, you can begin buying again as soon as the technical buy rules are intact. At least you have locked in some profits at a higher price. If, on the other hand, the stock begins climbing as soon as your trailing stop order triggers, you still own 150 shares (200- 50) of the original position to participate in the upward climb, and you've locked in a good profit on the shares that were sold. An addendum to this is one more point at which we recommend a stop. Since this is a conservative strategy, if the stock is within 10% of its highs and the PEG is above 2, the S4 system puts a stop on the stock. A PEG rate of 2 is fine for buying a stock below the 90% mark, but it begins raising a yellow flag for us when the price is high (within 90% of its 52-week high).

Trailing stop orders are great tools to use if you can't stare at the market and every stock you own all day, every day. If a black swan event happens to a stock and it suddenly drops, you and your financial advisor may not see it immediately. The stop order assures that at least part of your position will be sold in case of disaster. One note here. Our example shows us putting a 7% stop order on your stock. We have experimented over the years with 5% stops and 10% stops. Our conclusion is that the stocks are less likely to be stopped out with stops at 7% than 5%. This gives the stock a little extra range to float around until, hopefully, it continues its overall trend and begins climbing again. The extra 2% of downside is usually not enough to make a huge difference in your profits. On the other hand, a 10% stop can take a high enough percentage of your profit from you to make a difference that is felt financially. It may take the entire profit away. One other caveat is that if extremely bad news comes out about your company, the stock may immediately drop by more than your stop order percentage in one big trade. Once the price crosses your stop, it turns into a market order and will sell on the next trade. If you have a 7% stop order and the company has some bad news and goes down 12% in one trade, your order will execute at that point. So, suddenly you have sold at 12% below the high price instead of 7%. The stock may rally again after the market absorbs the news and begins trading above the price at which your shares sold. Or, it may continue to drop. That is the risk of protecting part of your profits with stop orders. It's not extremely common, but it needed to be discussed. That is also why we don't recommend putting a stop on more the 25% of your total position. Also, make sure your emotions are in check before entering the order. If the stock gets stopped out, you need to be able to say, "Great! That worked out as planned", instead of worrying about losing part of your investment. If you can't do that, you have met the definition of an emotional investor, and we refer you back to the section on emotional investing.

To recap the sell strategy:

1. Do not sell out an entire position at once.
2. Begin selling from highs if a stock is down 3 out of 4 days, including today, if the fundamental parameters aren't met.
3. Begin selling if the stock crosses below the most recent near-term low.

4. Start watching a stock very closely when the PEG rate goes above 3 be ready to begin pulling the trigger to sell if the price falls back.

5. Try not to sell a stock that meets the buying parameters unless it is selling for at least 90% of the 52-week high. Sometimes, a stock that is within the buying parameters will take a while to start moving or will stall out temporarily on the way up.

6. Sell in tranches of 25% of the total shares held.

7. If, after you sell a tranche or an entire position and the parameters improve, don't be afraid to begin a new position in the stock or add to the remaining position.

8. Begin selling if the stock falls through its 50- or 200-day moving average, if the stock does not meet the fundamental buying rules.

9. If a stock is within 10% of its highs and the fundamentals are still in place, you have three basic choices. One is to do nothing and hope it goes higher. The second choice is to sell 25% of the position and take some profits on part of your position. The third choice, which we prefer, is to put a 7% stop on 25% of the position. As mentioned above, you still give the stock a chance to continue its run-up, but you basically grab some insurance on part of the position in case it pulls back for unexpected reasons.

10. If a stock has run up to within 10% of its 52-week high and is still climbing, but no longer meets the fundamental rules, put a stop on 25% of the position.

11. If the stop executes in #10, you should either put another stop (since it has already executed once, the second stop should be 5%) on the position or go ahead and lighten another tranche of the position yourself. Since the fundamentals are no longer viable and the stock is moving down, there is little reason to hold it. Use the proceeds to buy a stock that meets our parameters.

Chapter 10

The Rating System

At this point, we have learned about fundamental analysis and technical analysis, and we have learned the rules for buying and selling and the logic behind them. The only thing left for us to do is to put this information together to form a usable, logical platform to use periodically to make our buying and selling decisions.

Travis went to work on the process several years ago and helped develop and computerize our great proprietary tool that we use daily to determine our buys and sells. In it, we look at all the stocks that we cover regularly (our universe). He has made a large part of the process automated, which saves time and reduces manual mistakes. The platform is being modified steadily as opportunities become available. We also keep a running history of buy and sell recommendations on each stock.

When I started developing the process, I would painstakingly go through my universe of stocks daily and handwrite the recommendations each day in a notebook. I have a pile of notebooks with this data that I have accumulated over the years until Travis computerized the process.

-Roy

Using the process in its current form, we look at each stock's fundamental and technical parameters and make the recommendation. These ratings are High, Buy, Sell, Pass, Lighten, and Stop Order. Each recommendation is only for that trading day since the situation may look different the next. It is a guide on what should be done that day. Having said that, I will point out that the direction of the recommendation rarely changes in a day's time.

Below are our recommendations and explanations:

A High rating is for stocks that are within 10% of their 52-week highs and are still within our parameters. They must have a PEG of 2 or less to be rated a high and not showing signs of turning down.

A Buy means that it should be accumulated now (remember, we buy in tranches, never all in at once). Buy signals mean that all of our parameters, technical and fundamental, are being met by the stock.

A sell means that it should be sold now (we rarely put a sell on a stock). Usually, if a stock is an outright sell, it is because earnings are expected to fall over the next couple of years, and the stock price has broken through all fundamental and technical support levels and needs to be sold immediately. It is also a sell if the company's business or management has created a situation that cannot be overcome within the next year, and that situation should drive the price down very soon. Another reason is if you have lost faith in the company's ability to grow its earnings, and the proceeds of the sale would be better used to buy a better stock with more upside potential and a buy rating. A fourth reason would be that the market itself is in a clear downturn. You would want to move out of any holdings with no fundamental or technical support. Those proceeds may be better placed, at that point, in a virtually risk-free money market or very short-term bond instrument until the market seems to be bottoming out or certain stocks appear to be bucking the market downtrend and consequently have a buy rating. Sometimes, the money market is the best investment.

A pass rating is usually used to represent a stock whose fundamentals are still in place, but the charts don't justify a buy recommendation. Sometimes a stock will have a nice run and then stall out for a few or even several sessions. We know it is a good company and feel like it will start moving again. However, large investors may see a potential problem in the future, and analysts are close to revising their earnings forecasts. In that case, it is prudent to put a pass on the stock and wait to see if the price starts moving again. At that time, if it begins moving up, we wait for the 3 out of 4 up days rule to materialize and start buying again. If, on the other hand, after the pause, the stock starts slipping down, we continue the pass rating until the fundamentals change or the stock drops below the support level. At this point, you should begin lightening up on the stock, or place a stop order on it in tranches as discussed earlier. A pass rating is also used to represent a stock that is running up but whose fundamentals don't justify the stock movement. We wouldn't want to start lightning up on the stock because we don't want to lose out on the price growth. Because the fundamentals aren't in place for it to be a buy, these stocks tend to be some of the riskiest. The investor doesn't want to let the stock go while it is running, because there may be a chance that analysts may increase the earnings projections. Conversely, any pullback in the market or misstep by the company can cause these stocks to drop drastically. We watch these stocks very closely. Any sign of the stock pausing its run or turning down in price would trigger us to lighten the position in tranches. So, items with a pass just mean we wouldn't buy them or sell them today, but we're keeping our eyes on them.

The third possible rating is a stop order (SO). We place stop orders on stocks in our universe that are high (within 10% of the 52-week high) that don't have the fundamentals currently to justify the stock price. We can also put a SO on a stock that is within 10% of the 52-week high, even if the stock appears fundamentally sound, but we are experiencing a volatile stock market, or the stock itself has been volatile recently. Remember, we see trailing stop orders as insurance policies with a 5% or 7% deductible.

We like to put them on a stock that's had a good run into that 10% area. Also, in volatile markets, we may put an SO on a stock that doesn't meet our parameters even if the stock is not within 10% of its highs. This can be done if the stock has 2 down days in a row. That could mean the beginning of a downturn.

We will place a lighten rating on a stock if we need to begin the selling process immediately. Again, we rarely sell out all of a position at once. If a stock is within 10% of the 52-week highs but has been slipping back, and the fundamentals are no longer supporting the stock, and a stop order would trigger the sale below that 10% zone, we can place a lighten rating on the stock. That would at least sell part of it above the 10% zone and theoretically guarantee a profit on that sale. If it keeps going down, we can lighten another tranche of the position. Try not to lighten a stock below the 10% zone unless your opinion of the company is such that you will not be tempted to buy it back within the next month. The reason for this is that sometimes, you may sell a tranche of a stock that is still fundamentally sound, and a few days later, it begins going up again and becomes a buy. Two situations can happen at this point. First, following the guidelines, you may want to or need to buy the stock back. If so, you will have PTSD (in investor terminology, that is Post Traumatic Stock Disorder), and it will chip away at your confidence to determine when to sell. The second situation occurs if your holding is outside of a retirement account, and you are selling at a loss. If you buy the stock back within 31 days, you may not be able to use the loss on your tax return. This is called the Wash Rule. However, you may be able to pick up that loss in the following trade. There are some nuances to this rule, and you should talk to your tax advisor to clarify your tax situation. Just be aware that the rule exists.

A snippet of our system is seen on the excerpt from the S4 decision page. It shows the results of a few days' ratings on a small portion of our final decision page. The stocks shown are not our entire universe of stocks followed, only the first few stocks alphabetically. Our entire stock universe is about 5 five times the size of this sample. It is not meant to be a recommendation or offer to buy or sell any stock as you are reading this. It only shows our recommendations on the days shown in 2025. Situations and ratings change from day to day. The period shown was an interesting time when the market was in turmoil while deciding what the new Trump Tariffs would mean to stocks. Review our discussion of emotional investing. You can see that at the first of this period, there were more stocks that filtered through the S4 as buys. As time went on and emotions ran raw, prices began slipping, and trailing stop orders were required to protect investments if these negative investor emotions continued. Most of these stops were on stocks that had high PEG rates. Some were on stock that may have passed our fundamental analysis, but the price action merited the insurance that a trailing stop order afforded on a portion of the position.

Remember, your universe of stocks to watch may be different than ours. You have built your own investment universe.

Excerpt from the S4 Decision Page

Symbol	Price	PEG	52 wk high	10% mark	4/29/2025	4/30/2025	5/1/2025	5/5/2025	5/9/2025	5/13/2025	5/14/2025	5/15/2025	5/16/2025	5/19/2025	5/20/2025	5/21/2025	5/22/2025	5/23/2025
STOCK 1	247.66	4.26	260.10	234.09	pass	so	pass	so	pass	pass	pass	pass	pass	so	so	so	so	so
STOCK 2	230.3	1.33	244.81	220.33	pass	so	pass	buy	pass	pass	so	pass	pass	buy	pass	pass	pass	pass
STOCK 3	339.32	1.06	557.90	502.11	buy	pass	buy	buy	buy	pass	buy	buy	buy	buy	pass	pass	pass	pass
STOCK 4	129.54	2.40	246.19	221.57	pass	so	pass	pass	pass	buy	pass	pass	so	pass	so	pass	pass	pass
STOCK 5	219.48	2.62	226.49	203.84	pass	pass	pass	pass	buy	buy	buy	buy	so	so	so	pass	pass	pass
STOCK 6	216.42	0.95	240.10	216.09	buy	so	buy	pass	buy	buy	buy	pass	buy	pass	pass	pass	pass	pass
STOCK 7	292.405	4.12	335.88	302.29	pass	so	so	so	pass	pass	t	so	pass	pass	pass	so	so	so
STOCK 8	45.45	#N/A	53.24	47.92	so	so	pass	high	high	high	pass	high	high	so	pass	pass	high	high
STOCK 9	220.07	2.06	242.52	218.27	pass	so	pass	pass	buy	buy	pass	pass	pass	pass	so	so	pass	pass
STOCK 10	590.11	1.29	745.61	671.05	buy	so	buy	buy	buy	buy	buy	pass	buy	buy	pass	pass	pass	pass
STOCK 11	87.77	#N/A	92.65	83.39	buy	so	pass	buy	pass	buy	buy	pass	pass	pass	pass	pass	pass	so
STOCK 12	52.87	0.91	61.25	55.13	buy	pass	pass	pass	pass	buy	buy	pass	pass	pass	so	so	so	t
STOCK 13	356.7	1.21	374.23	336.81	pass	so	buy	buy	buy	high	high	high	high	high	high	high	high	high
STOCK 14	710	3.12	885.91	797.32	so	so	so	so	so	so	so	so	so	so	so	so	so	so
STOCK 15	186.66	1.72	251.99	226.79	Sell	Sell	Sell	Sell	Sell	Sell	Sell	Sell	Sell	Sell	Sell	Sell	Sell	Sell
STOCK 16	491.93	#N/A	542.07	487.86	so	so	so	so	so	so	so	so	pass	pass	pass	pass	so	so
STOCK 17	52.31	4.66	86.88	78.19	pass	so	pass	pass	so	so	so	so	so	so	so	so	pass	so
STOCK 18	504.76	3.29	511.50	460.35	buy	pass	buy	buy	pass	buy	pass	pass	buy	pass	pass	pass	pass	pass
STOCK 19	28.09	0.53	32.80	29.52	pass	pass	pass	buy	buy	buy	buy	buy	buy	pass	pass	pass	pass	pass
STOCK 20	40.9	2.65	66.74	60.07	pass	so	so	pass	pass	so	pass	pass	pass	pass	pass	so	so	so
STOCK 21	356.99	#N/A	444.64	400.18	pass	so	pass	so	so	so	pass	so	buy	pass	pass	so	so	so
STOCK 22	88.78	10.77	115.38	103.84	so	so	pass	pass	so	so	so	so	so	so	so	so	so	so
STOCK 23	935.56	5.07	1078.23	970.41	so	so	so	so	so	so	so	so	so	so	so	so	so	so
STOCK 24	56.31	#N/A	61.92	55.73	buy	pass	pass	pass	buy	buy	pass	pass	pass	pass	pass	pass	pass	so

Chapter 11

Putting It All Together

We have now been through the basic stages of our stock analysis. We have our list of the universe of stocks we will follow, we know the fundamental analysis of finding PEG rates and deciding which stocks we should even begin considering buying, and we have learned the intricacies of determining which in that group of elite stocks passes our screen on a technical basis and should be bought now.

As mentioned before, this proprietary system was originally entered by hand by Roy every day for years before Travis developed the program we use on the computer. While the fundamental analysis is performed within his program, a lot of the technical analysis is still done manually because it is more of an art than a science.

We would recommend that you do the fundamental analysis by hand at first. It will help you get used to the process through daily or weekly repetition. You will get faster as time goes on. Basically, you just need to make a list of your universe of stocks placed vertically on the left side of a spreadsheet. Date each column at the top. As you go down your list, rate each stock as a buy, sell, pass, lighten, or stop order as you go through your fundamental and technical analysis of each. The next time you go through the list, go to the next column and do the same analysis on each stock, marking your rating for that day. Repeat the same process every period you choose to do the analysis. We recommend you try to do it regularly and not hit and miss. Over time, looking back at the spreadsheet you have kept, you will see patterns emerge that can be used to solidify your faith in the process and the convictions of the purchases and sales that you make. Some stocks will stay at a pass rating for quite a while until one day you start seeing the pattern fall into place as a buy emerges for the stock. Of course, you may also know the sell patterns as they emerge. The visibility of the patterns is good and will help you make your decisions. Just follow the rules of the Sparkman Stock Selection System (S4).

If, on the other hand, you decide that it is too time-consuming for you, we have a simple suggestion for you. At the risk of shameless self-promotion, if you would prefer to open an account with us, you can piggyback off our daily analysis. We will make the recommendations to you as needed and make the trades for you in your account with us. This will save you a lot of time and allow you to go on with the more important things in your life. In the process of opening the account, we can also put together a financial plan for you.

In this way, we help clients determine their financial hopes, dreams, and fears as well as their risk analysis. This helps us to help you turn your financial dreams into reality. Our phone number and email address are at the end of the book.

Chapter 12

Closed-End Funds

The preceding chapters show the process we go through to determine our stock recommendations. It can also be used to analyze the potential for investing in certain other investments that are traded on major exchanges. One investment type that we watch and in which we invest when the opportunity appears is closed-end funds (also known as CEFs).

To explain this type of investment, one must understand the concept of mutual funds in general. Most investors have invested in mutual funds. If you are one of the few who think they haven't invested in funds, just look at your 401 (k) retirement account. Most of the investments offered inside of 401Ks are mutual funds. Even though most adults own at least some shares directly or indirectly (through 401Ks), most investors don't really understand how mutual funds work.

A mutual fund is basically a company that, instead of making and selling widgets, buys stock in other companies. The investors in the fund all share in the ownership of the companies in which the fund invests. Their ownership of the shares of the companies that the fund buys is prorated proportionately to the percentage of the fund's total shares that the fund has issued to date.

Let's illustrate this in a very simplistic example. Mutual fund ABC buys shares of large growth companies. There are 5 investors. Investor 1 has invested $1,000 in the fund. Investor 2 has invested $2,000; Investor 3 has invested $3,000, Investor 4 has invested $4,000, and Investor 5 has invested $5,000. That is a total investment of $15,000 into the fund. ABC issues its initial shares at $10 each for 1,500 shares.

Investor 1 owns 6.66% ($1,000/$15,000) of the shares., Investor 2 owns 13.32% ($2,000/$15,000) of the shares, and so on to Investor 5, who owns 33.33% ($5,000/$15,000). The fund takes the deposits and buys equal dollar ($7,500 each) amounts of Software Company and Cola Company, two companies that it feels will do well. At the end of the market day a year later, the stocks have gone up an average of 10%. The fund prices its shares. The investments inside the fund are now worth $16,500, and there are still 1,500 shares. The fund's share price goes up to $11 per share ($16,500/1500 shares). So, each investor in the fund has a capital gain of 10%. Now, take this illustration and multiply it by billions of dollars, millions of investors, and 30 to 50 stock positions, and that is a basic picture of how all mutual funds work.

New shares in open-end funds may be issued daily, depending on whether new investors are buying into the fund. To continue the example, the next day, a new person becomes interested in fund ABC. Her name is Investor 6, and she wants to invest $1,500 into the fund. For ease of illustration, assume the market was flat that day and the underlying investments didn't move up or down.

The shares are now selling at $11 per share. Investor 6 receives 136.36 shares ($1,500 investment/$11 per share). So, now the fund has total investments of $18,000 (the original shares are worth a total of $16,500, and the new investment is $1,500). The fund decides it wants to add another stock, Pharmaceutical Company, to its portfolio, but wants to own equal dollars of each stock that it owns. So, it sells a small amount of the Software Company and the Cola Company and buys some of the Pharmaceutical Company so that the position in each stock is now worth $6,000.

There are now 6 investors. Investor 1 now owns 6.11% ($1,100/$18,000) of the total value of the fund, and investor 6 owns 8.33% ($1,500/$18000). The other investors also own their proportionate share of the total value. This calculation determines the fund's Net Asset Value (NAV) at the close of the market each day. All mutual funds determine their net asset value in this way.

There are two types of mutual funds, open-end and closed-end. It is important to know the difference between the two. There are differences between open-end and closed-end funds. When one buys an open-end fund, he/she is buying shares from the fund. The fund issues more shares to buyers or buys back shares from investors who need to sell. The shares are not traded on any stock exchange. All trades are made at Net Asset Value at the end of the market day. Most funds will add a reasonable load (commission) to the purchase amount. If so, there is no charge when the fund is sold.

On the other hand, shares of closed-end funds are traded on major stock exchanges, and there is a fixed number of shares that have been issued and are traded constantly during the trading day, just like any security. Therefore, when you buy a closed-end fund, you are effectively buying shares of the fund from an investor who wants to sell the shares, just as is the process when you buy shares of a stock. The transactions are facilitated by a broker who is a member of the stock exchange on which the shares are traded. Because of this constant public buying and selling of the shares, the price of the closed-end fund can and does change several times per day. However, as previously mentioned, the NAV or net asset value of the fund is determined after the market closes. Since the shares of these funds are traded constantly and the NAV is determined at the end of the day, a disparity usually exists between the two values. At times, the market price of close-end funds can trade at a premium to the NAV. At other times, it can trade at a discount to NAV. Our strategy looks for shares of closed-end funds that are trading at a minimum 10% discount to their NAV. In this way, at the point of purchase, it feels like we are buying a dollar bill for 90 cents or less. A lot of times, a closed-end fund will trade at a discount for quite a while, and then, if it begins moving up in price at a faster rate than NAV, that discount to NAV will get smaller and smaller, and at some point, the price may go to a premium. Ideally, the time to sell is when the closed-end fund goes to a premium of 5 to 10% of NAV.

Another reason to buy a closed-end fund at a discount is its ability to convert, with the majority of shareholders' permission, to an open-end fund. As it changes to open-end status, it will automatically sell at NAV permanently (just like all open-end funds), thereby giving you a nice bump in price and profit. This is the fundamental analysis we do for mutual funds. Of course, we also do our technical analysis and use the same technical parameters as we do for any other equity. Another characteristic of closed-end funds is that some of them can use small amounts of margin to buy more shares of the stocks in which they invest. Also, some closed-end funds pay a high dividend that is a set % of the value of the NAV of the fund. Some of these higher dividends can be achieved with the leverage that the fund uses, as well as returning capital gains that the fund has taken, or out of principle. Some of these funds may pay out cash flow to investors of as much as 7% or more. Since they pay a higher dividend, some investors use them as an income alternative with appreciation potential. There are also closed-end funds that invest in corporate bonds and tax-free municipal funds. The analysis of these funds is done in the same manner as equity-based closed-end funds. The reader must understand that the NAV of all mutual funds can move up or down daily as the market moves, and there is always a chance of loss as well as gain.

You can find a list of closed-end mutual funds by Googling "list of closed-end funds." It will give recent prices and NAVs for the funds. These prices aren't current since the funds trade constantly, and the NAVs are priced each day. There are so many that it would be better to talk to a financial advisor who works regularly with closed-end funds to suggest some that meet your needs and investment profile.

Given the above dissertation about closed-end funds, it is also prudent for us to mention that we also like open-end funds and use them regularly. However, occasionally, an individual closed-end fund can give unique buying opportunities. Several closed-end funds are in our universe of stocks that we go through daily, but they are a different type of security, and we analyze them using discounts to NAV (as discussed earlier) instead of PEG rates. We still use the up three out of 4- up-day rule before we buy.

Chapter 13

Working with a Financial Advisor

Admittedly, we are biased, have strong egos, and have enough confidence in the hundreds of Financial Advisors we have had the privilege to know over the years, that we are comfortable saying that investors, potentially, can have better performance by working with a financial professional. Now that we have stated our bias, we will point out that numerous studies support our conclusion.

A white paper titled "Self-Investing Versus Advice," written by Yodeler and published February 7, 2023, discusses studies done by Vanguard and the Financial Conduct Authority. These studies found that Investors who used Financial Advisors earned returns that averaged 3% more per year than those who invested without an advisor. Bear in mind that these returns were after the additional cost of the advisor was factored in. This is just one article about one study. Bear in mind that not all advisors or results are typical.

Factors that lead to the overperformance by advised accounts are that the advisors helped the investors reduce the likelihood of making emotional decisions (creative irrationality) and buying higher risk investments. They also had the ability and tools available to help the clients plan an investment strategy suited to the investor's unique circumstances.

Individual investors tend to jump into stocks after the stock has already run up because of FOMO (Fear of Missing Out) when the financial news broadcasts have touted the stock's performance. Usually, by the time the broadcasters talk about a stock's performance, it is too late to buy. The studies also showed that individual investors tend to sell gainers too early and hold on to losing positions for too long. A good financial advisor should discourage this behavior if appropriate. Sometimes, in fact, a pullback in price of a sound stock is a buying opportunity, and the advisor might recommend a buy as opposed to the investor's emotional desire to sell. There is a unique phenomenon that we have observed about the brokerage industry that is different from any others. If a retailer, such as Macy's, puts its merchandise on sale at a 20% discount, customers will flock in to buy the merchandise.

Conversely, if the stock market falls by 20% very few people will buy a stock. The stock market, at this point, is on sale and no one will touch it. If the market rallies and goes to new highs, financial advisors receive numerous calls from investors that want in. This is emotional investing. Buy low and sell high is an investment rule that is intuitive but counter emotional.

We borrowed part of our investment philosophy from a good gardener: "Pull the weeds and let the flowers grow through their season." Sell the stocks that no longer have good fundamentals and technicals, and let the winners have their chance to grow.

Individual investors, according to the studies, tend to gravitate to lower-priced stocks. These stocks tend to have a great story, but sometimes lack fundamentals and can be very volatile. Advisors strive to tend the investors to successful companies and increase the likelihood of success. These stocks may seem more expensive, but the risk-to-reward ratio may be much better.

Another advantage to working with advisors is that they have the experience and tools needed for financial planning to help the client set financial goals and strategies to meet their needs.

So, how significant is the extra 3% that the article said one might earn by using a Financial Advisor? Let's suppose that you started investing with $250,000. You invested this yourself without assistance from an advisor for 15 years. Assume your average return is 5% annualized for that time. Congratulations, you grew your principle substantially. Over the past 15 years, you increased your investments from $250,000 to $519,732. Pat yourself on the back. Now, suppose you used a good Financial Advisor for that same period, and he was good enough to earn you the extra 3% return that the studies have shown. Over the same 15-year period, he would have given you a total of 8% (5%+3%value added) annualized return. This would have meant that your principle would have grown from $250,000 to $793,042.

That is a value added of $273,310 ($793,042-$519,732) or over 52.5% extra over the 15 years. That extra earnings would have been more than your original principle. How significant is that to you? Obviously, this illustration is hypothetical, and there are no guarantees that your results would be the same. All in all, we believe these studies show that using advisors in your investments may give you better performance and confidence in your investment decisions.

At this point, let's assume that you have decided to use a Financial Advisor to help you with your investments. Here are the things you should look for in the advisors that you interview. We would recommend these questions in this order.

1. Do they recommend individual stocks regularly in their business, or do they only recommend package products (mutual funds, unit trusts, annuities, etc.)?

2. If they recommend their clients invest in stocks, can they give you their top 5 stocks that they would recommend for a moderate risk client today?
3. Do they have a written process or system for picking stocks, and ask them to summarize that system to you. This is critical. If they don't have a written process or can't summarize it to you in a clear manner that you can understand, that should send up a red flag. If they can give you their system, does their logic make sense to you? Does the math work?
4. Now ask them to go back to the stocks recommended in question 2 and show you how they fit into their stock selection system. Make sure those stocks match their process. If not, a yellow or red flag should be flying in your head.
5. If they don't have a process, this book would make a great gift to them
6. Buy in small tranches until your target investment is reached. It's never all in at once.

Chapter 14

Commission or Fee-Based Accounts

While investing with a financial advisor, one will at some point need to decide on the form of payment for financial services. There are, basically, two options. These are commissions per trade and fee-based.

The commission per trade is, as the name implies, paying a small commission for each trade made. Usually, these commissions on average-sized equity transactions will run between 1½% 2%. This can vary to some extent depending on the size of trades. Larger trades are usually charged a smaller percentage than smaller trades. There is usually a minimum dollar commission charged for small trades. The minimum commission varies from broker to broker, but one can expect it to run around $40. Even though we recommend buying bite-sized tranches of a position you are trying to accumulate, we think that the minimum purchase on a trade is about $2,000. If the minimum commission is

$40, that would cost you 2% to make the trade. As we have stated earlier, we want investors to enter a position expecting to make at least a 10% profit over the next year. Obviously, some trades will move faster and farther than that. Even if the gross profit on a trade is only 10%, paying a 2% commission to buy and 2% to sell would still give a net profit of 6%. If you were able to repeat this trade a few times per year, you might be able to accumulate a sizeable percentage profit on the same dollars over the year. We use this example only as an illustration to show that even small investors can grow their assets without being overly concerned about commissions. A small trade to add to other small trades to accumulate a larger position in a stock is even better. It should grow to an even larger amount. Therefore, commissions from future sales of tranches from the larger position might be made at a lower percentage commission.

Some investors spend an inordinate amount of time and energy worrying about commissions. All in all, commissions just aren't a major part of the overall picture when using the S4 to pick your trades. One of the most frustrating things that we have heard as advisors is that paying a 1 1/2 or 2% commission on a trade is too high. Really? What about the 15 or 20% tip (or another way to look at it is commission) you paid to the waiter in the restaurant where you last ate? Basically, you paid him a commission to write the order for the lunch that you were going to buy in the first place. What about the 6% total commission you paid to sell your house? We're not saying that anyone who performs these services is overpaid; we're just trying to put things into perspective. Transactions have costs, and the reality is that a high proportion of the commission you pay goes to the brokerage firm for processing the order and paying the overhead. A small amount of that is netted by the advisor. But we digress and will now come down from our high horses.

Fee-based accounts are charged annual fees for the accounts. Trades in the account are usually done with no commission charged to the client. The fees are charged to compensate the firm and advisor in lieu of commissions. Usually, one quarter of the annual fee is charged quarterly, in advance of the quarter. To get a better picture of this, assume you open a $200,000 fee-based account that charges you 2%. When you open the account, it will be charged 0.5% (one quarter of the agreed-upon fee) when the account is opened. The dollar amount of the beginning fee would be $1,000 (.005 X $200,000). The financial advisor or portfolio manager enters the trades when they meet the parameters of their investment system. At the beginning of the second quarter, another fee of .5% is charged based on the value of the account at that point. Let's say the market was down for the first quarter and the value of the account fell to $190,000. The fee would be $950 ($190,000 x .005). Then the market has a nice rally, and the value is $210,000 at the beginning of the third quarter. The fee for that quarter would still be .5% but it is based on the higher value of $210,000 or $1050. Each quarter's fee is based on .5% of the value of the account at the beginning of the quarter. The percent of the fee can vary from one account to another. The variance can be based on the value of the account (a $1,000,000 account would have a lower percentage fee than a $50,000 account). The range in variation of fees is usually between 1% to 3%.

The fee-based accounts can be managed entirely by the advisor at his discretion based on his strategy, as agreed upon by the client. Otherwise, the account can be managed by the advisor, with each trade individually being approved by the client. This can create a problem if the client can't be located at the time a trade needs to be placed. Since the trade can't be made without the client's permission, critical opportunities may be missed. We prefer the discretionary account as a means to eliminate this problem. The advisor can make the trade when it needs to be made without the prior approval of the client. Also, using a set process takes the emotions out of the trade. As we have discussed, emotional trading is suboptimal. The other reason for discretionary advisor-managed accounts is that some trades need to be made quickly when market conditions create a buying window. We and every other Private Wealth Manager have had problems at one time or another trying to reach the clients when such opportunities arise. The trade may not be made if the account is set up on a non-discretionary basis and the client can't be reached. For these reasons, we recommend this type of account be set up with discretion. The client can always give input on types of investments that are not to be considered or those that are preferred.

Just as a side note, another type of fee-based account that has worked well for clients is a Separately Managed Account. These SMA, as they are known, are usually managed by large, successful Management Companies that specialize in such types of accounts. Most of them require minimum starting account sizes of $1,000,000 or more and are inaccessible to most retail investors. Most brokerage firms, however, have agreements with these large managers by which a retail investor can open accounts that these mega managers manage for as small an account as $100,000. The fees are usually a little higher but within the previously mentioned fee ranges. These are not mutual funds, and each trade and position will show up in the client's monthly statements. There are many managers for this type of account. Some are consistently good performers, and some are not. Most good advisors will have experience with this type of account and can help you set up accounts with managers with whom they have a proven track record of success. We have narrowed our focus, through experience over the years, to about 6 that have earned our recommendation. These accounts are totally discretionary for the portfolio managers. The client gets little input, but at times that's a good thing. Just relax and let your advisor keep an eye on your account and regularly report back to you. We only mention them here because they buy individual stocks, and that is what this book is about. SMAs can be excellent investment vehicles for a client who wants to have sound investments but doesn't feel the need to be involved in the investment decision process. You do need to have a good, experienced advisor who can vet the different managers and advise you on which ones would meet your financial needs and profile. We should also mention that there are SMAs that invest their portfolios in bonds, also. This allows clients to diversify their portfolios between bonds and equities.

Chapter 15

Recap the System

Now you have it. You've gone through the basics of the Sparkman Stock Selection System. It is an easily understandable, easily replicable, concise, successful, and elegant plan that will help you pick your stocks for your investment portfolio.

Just to review the process:

1) Keep your universe of stocks that you watch regularly limited to 75 to 150 companies with which you are familiar.
2) Choose the stocks of companies from this list that are currently profitable. They will have a Price to Earnings ratio (P/E)
3) From this group, choose the stocks that have rising projected earnings according to the mean estimate of the analysts following the company.
4) Calculate the PEG ratio (price/earnings/growth) of the stocks in this group and look for a PEG ratio of under 3. The lower the PEG, the better.
5) Of the stocks with a PEG of under 3, pick the stocks that have been up 3 of the past 4 trading sessions or have recently gone above either the 50-day or 200-

day moving average, or have recently gone above a near-term peak.

6) The stocks that have survived this Stock Selection Funnel are your buys.

The selling funnel is just the opposite.

1. In selling, lightening up on stocks or stop orders, the technical analysis usually trumps the fundamental analysis within reason. Start lightening stocks that have recently traded below the most recent near-term low or broken below the 50-day or 200-day moving average.
2. Of these positions with deteriorating technicals, look for stocks that you own with a PEG above 3
3. If these stocks are within 10% of their highs, put a stop of 5 to 7% on them. Even a stock within the 10% range with a PEG of as low as 2 should have a trailing stop order.
4. If the stock is below 90% of its 52-week high and drops below one of the previously discussed support levels, it might be time to lighten your position. Move out of positions in 25% increments.
5. After you have lightened a couple of times and the stock still has good fundamentals, put a pass on it. You should still hold the remainder of the position, but at that point, you leave it alone until the technicals start looking more favorable, even if it continues to drop. Eventually, investors with level heads realize the fundamental value of the stock

and begin buying again. A lot of times, this will occur as the stocks hit a low level from which they bounced previously and then begin to rise.

6. At that point, go back to the buying parameters to determine whether the stock is a buy.

Chapter 16

A Couple of Extra Charts to Study Just for Fun

We've discussed ad nauseam some technical analysis that you should understand to get a feel for judging investor emotions. You should understand waiting for 3 out of 4 consecutive up days before buying, assuming the fundamentals are in place for the security stock. You should also have a feel for the effects that the 50 and 200-day averages, as well as breaking through recent highs or lows, have on a stock.

Here are a couple of stock patterns that are interesting to look for. Both patterns are touted in most technical analysis books as being effective, so we have included them. There are never guarantees on the results of these or any other patterns, but they can serve as rules of thumb.

The first pattern to look at is the inverted head and shoulders pattern. This can be seen in the shorter-term ABC Chart 4 on the page 115. ABC met our fundamental parameters at the time of the chart. Sometimes these patterns require you to use your goofy eye to see. You should be able to see the shape of a person standing on the tip of his/her head. If you are having trouble with it, turn the book upside down and take a look. As the chart moves down the torso of the body, you can see a series of lower lows and lower highs until August 6th, 2024. At that point, it rallies slightly until the 20th. And then continues down until it bottoms on September 10th. Now touch your own shoulder and head to your neck. That soft part between your shoulder joint and your neck is what we would call the bottom of the shoulder. That soft area of your shoulder coincides with the August 20th point on the chart. Remember, you are upside down. The low point of the chart (August 14th) coincides with the tip of your head. From the tip of the head, the chart begins rising again until October 4th. That is the bottom of the other shoulder. It then pulls back until October 10th, at which time it turns up again and begins to retrace the opposite side of the torso. Now here is the mathematical theory. The bottoms of both shoulders line up almost perfectly. We have drawn a horizontal line between the bottom of both shoulders. The distance from that line to the tip of the head is 19 points (168.5-149.5). In theory, the run that should take place from that line has the potential to rise by the same distance from the tip of the head to that line. So, add 19 points to 168.5. The target top of the current run may go at least as high as 187.5. Again, this is theory, and some people swear by it. They might start buying when the price goes above the line. Since you are now an astute investor, using the

S4, you would have bought a tranche on September 12th, which would be the first 3 out of 4 up day moves.

In fact, our records show that we purchased on that day. You would also buy as it crossed the 50-day moving average and the 200-day moving average. There are several points between these averages at which other tranches could be purchased.

But, back to the Inverted Head and Shoulders chart. It predicted that the run could go as high as 187.5. We ran the chart again on February 1st (Chart 5) and found that ABC went up from 187.5 to 207.47. That is a bonus return above expectations of $20 per share.

Chart 4

ABC
©StockCharts.com
15-Nov-2024 Op 175.24 Hi 175.48 Lo 172.35 Last 173.50 Vol 21.7M Chg -3.45 (-1.95%)
ABC (Daily) 173.50 (15 Nov)
MA(50) 166.63
MA(200) 164.13
Volume 21,735,500
Expected price 19 points above shoulder 187
Bottom of Shoulder
19 Points
Top of Head
173.50
166.63
164.13
15 22 29 Aug 12 19 26 Sep 9 16 23 Oct 7 14 21 28 Nov 11

Chart 5

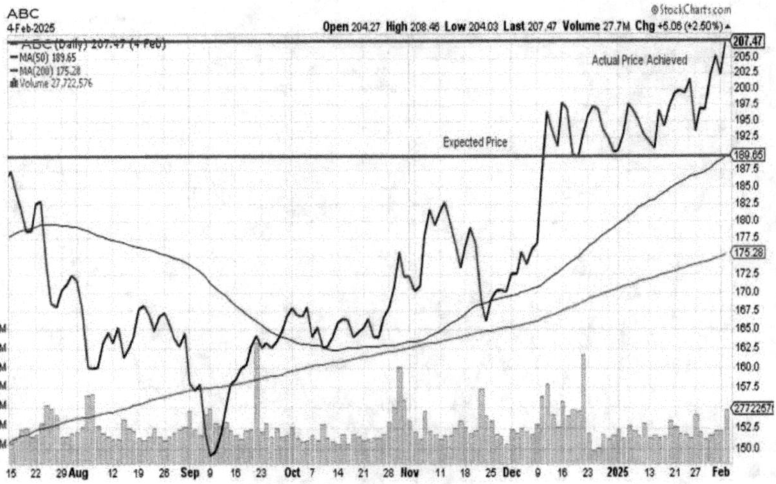

ABC
4-Feb-2025
©StockCharts.com
Open 204.27 High 208.46 Low 204.03 Last 207.47 Volume 27.7M Chg +5.06 (+2.50%)
ABC (Daily) 207.47 (4 Feb)
MA(50) 189.65
MA(200) 175.28
Volume 27,722,576
Actual Price Achieved
Expected Price
207.47
189.65
175.28
15 22 29 Aug 12 19 26 Sep 9 16 23 Oct 7 14 21 28 Nov 11 18 25 Dec 9 16 23 2025 13 21 27 Feb

Another chart that seems to be popular is the cup and handle chart. It is represented by Chart 6 of stock 123 on page 119. The stock met our fundamental parameters at the time of this chart. Visualize a coffee cup. You should be able to see the deep bowl and its handle. In this chart, you can see the formation of the cup beginning on June 27th at 102, as it begins its deep drop, it forms the left side of the cup. On August 13th, it bottoms out at 86, and on the 14th, it begins its ascent up the right side to 96. However, its upward trajectory stalls on October 1st as it pulls back for a few days to 92before climbing again. This is the beginning of the cup handle. Eventually, the handle climbs until it crosses the horizontal line we have drawn from the point at which the handle began. The price of the stock at that point is 96. Similar to the inverted head and shoulders in the previous chart, a true technical proponent would begin buying as the chart crossed that line. Also, the distance from the bottom of the cup to that line would, theoretically, be the potential distance that the stock could run above that line. That distance is 15 points. Therefore, theoretically, the stock could run 15 points above the price where the handle began. So, the run could bring the stock up to 111 (96+15). This is technical analysis at its rawest. There are no guarantees of performance. Like the ABC example, we feel that a true technician would have left quite a bit of profit on the table. Using the S4 system, the first buying point (3 out of 4 up days) would have been on

August 16th at 89. There were multiple buying points along the way, including September 17th as it crossed the 50-day moving average and any 3 out of 4 up day marks as it regained from a minor pullback. Even though these charts are theoretical, it can be fun to watch for these patterns.

Just a side note. We printed these charts on the dates that they appear. It is interesting to note that, as seen on Chart 7, by Christmas Eve, the stock had not only passed the 111 point but exceeded it to approximately 117 before beginning a pullback. That's an excess bonus return of $6 per share.

Chart 6

123 NYSE + BATS
© StockCharts.com
15-Nov-2024 Open 109.76 High 114.68 Low 109.76 Last 114.57 Volume 32.1M Chg +5.93 (+5.46%)
123 (Daily) 114.57 (15 Nov)
MA(50) 95.14
MA(200) 100.78
Volume 32,138,612
15 Point Expected profit to 111
Beginning of Handle 96
15 Points
81
114.57
100.78
95.14
321386
112
110
108
106
104
102
100
98
96
94
92
88
86
50M
40M
30M
20M
10M
24
Jul
8
15
22
29
Aug
12
19
26
Sep
9
16
23
Oct
7
14
21
28
Nov
11

Chart 7

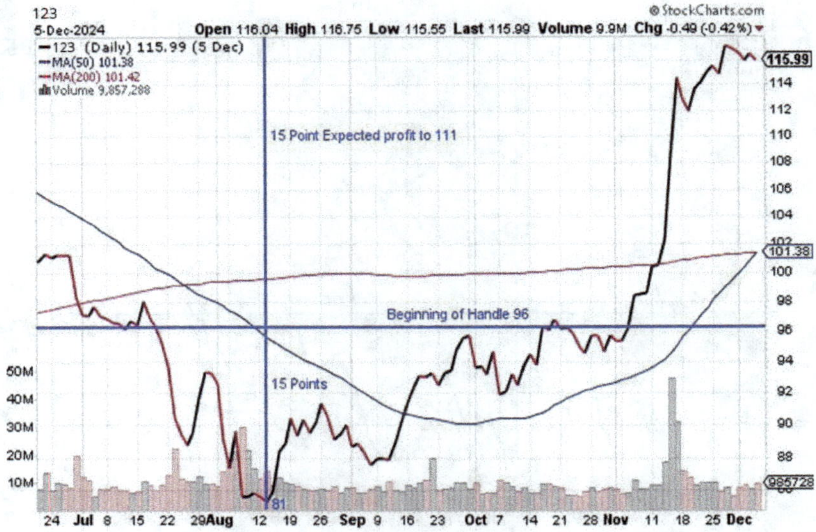
123
5-Dec-2024
Open 116.04 High 116.75 Low 115.55 Last 115.99 Volume 9.9M Chg -0.49 (-0.42%)
© StockCharts.com
123 (Daily) 115.99 (5 Dec)
MA(50) 101.38
MA(200) 101.42
Volume 9,857,288
15 Point Expected profit to 111
Beginning of Handle 96
15 Points
81
115.99
101.38
24 Jul 8 15 22 29 Aug 12 19 26 Sep 9 16 23 Oct 7 14 21 28 Nov 11 18 25 Dec

For further reading, the book Technical Analysis of Stock Trends by Robert Edwar, John Magee, and WHC Bassetti has been called by some to be the Bible of technical analysis.

Chapter 17

Conclusion

The above gives you the needed parameters for the Sparkman Stock Selection System (S4). It should be easy for current or potential investors to understand. If you think it makes sense to you, please recommend it or give a copy to a friend or financial advisor.

If you would like to have a Wealth Manager help you with your investments, please give us a call at 512-676-5999 or go to our website, sparkmanswm.com.

So, that's our little book that has the potential to help you create big financial results. Now it's up to you.

Therefore, go forth and multiply...your investments!

The End

Disclosures

The information contained in this book does not purport to be a complete description of the securities, markets, or developments referred to in this material. The information has been obtained from sources considered to be reliable, but we do not guarantee that the foregoing material is accurate or complete. Any information is not a complete summary or statement of all available data necessary for making an investment decision and does not constitute a recommendation. Any opinions are those of the author and not necessarily those of RJFS or Raymond James. Expressions of opinion are as of the initial book publishing date and are subject to change without notice.

Raymond James is not affiliated with and does not endorse the opinions or services of any organizations, authors, and sources mentioned herein.

Certified Financial Planner Board of Standards, Inc. (CFP Board) owns the certification marks CFP®, CERTIFIED FINANCIAL PLANNER™, and CFP® (with plaque design) in the United States, which it authorizes use of by individuals who successfully complete CFP Board's initial and ongoing certification requirements.

Bond prices and yields are subject to change based upon market conditions and availability. If bonds are sold prior to maturity, you may receive more or less than your initial investment. There is an inverse relationship between interest rate movements and fixed income prices. Generally, when interest rates rise, fixed income prices fall and when interest rates fall, fixed income prices rise.

Indices are not available for direct investment. Any investor who attempts to mimic the performance of an index would incur fees and expenses which would reduce returns.

The S&P 500 is an unmanaged index of 500 widely held stocks that is generally considered representative of the U.S. stock market.

Bitcoin issuers are not registered with the SEC, and the bitcoin marketplace is currently unregulated. Bitcoin and other cryptocurrencies are a very speculative investment and involves a high degree of risk.

Bond prices and yields are subject to change based upon market conditions and availability. If bonds are sold prior to maturity, you may receive more or less than your initial investment. There is an inverse relationship between interest rate movements and fixed income prices. Generally, when interest rates rise, fixed income prices fall and when interest rates fall, fixed income prices rise.

U.S. government bonds and Treasury notes are guaranteed by the U.S. government and, if held to maturity, offer a fixed rate of return and guaranteed principal value. U.S. government bonds are issued and guaranteed as to the timely payment of principal and interest by the federal government. Treasury notes are certificates reflecting intermediate-term (2 - 10 years) obligations of the U.S. government.

Gold is subject to the special risks associated with investing in precious metals, including but not limited to: price may be subject to wide fluctuation; the market is relatively limited; the sources are concentrated in countries that have the potential for instability; and the market is unregulated.

In a fee-based account clients pay a quarterly fee, based on the level of assets in the account, for the services of a financial advisor as part of an advisory relationship. In deciding to pay a fee rather than commissions, clients should understand that the fee may be higher than a commission alternative during periods of lower trading. Advisory fees are in addition to the internal expenses charged by mutual funds and other investment company securities. To the extent that clients intend to hold these securities, the internal expenses should be included when evaluating the costs of a fee-based account. Clients should periodically re-evaluate whether the use of an asset-based fee continues to be appropriate in servicing their needs. A list of additional considerations, as well as the fee schedule, is available in the firm's Form ADV Part 2 as well as the client agreement.

Securities offered through Raymond James Financial Services, Inc., member FINRA / SIPC. Investment advisory services offered through Raymond James Financial Services Advisors, Inc. Sparkman Wealth Management is not a registered broker/dealer and is independent of Raymond James Financial Services.

Travis Sparkman, Owner and Financial Advisor

Roy Sparkman CFP®

Sparkman Wealth Management

13706 Research Blvd Suite 306

Austin Tx 78750

512-676-5999

sparkmanswm.com

www.ingramcontent.com/pod-product-compliance
Lightning Source LLC
LaVergne TN
LVHW022100200926
848481LV00003B/1011
9798896046011